THE GOSPEL FOR KIDS

Series C

ELDON WEISHEIT

Publishing House
St. Louis

Other books by Eldon Weisheit:
61 Worship Talks for Children
61 Gospel Talks for Children
Excuse Me, Sir
The Zeal of His House
The Preacher's Yellow Pants
Moving
To the Kid in the Pew, Series A
To the Kid in the Pew, Series B
To the Kid in the Pew, Series C
The Gospel for Kids, Series A
The Gospel for Kids, Series B

The Scripture quotations in this publication are from the Good News Bible, The Bible in Today's English Version. Copyright © TEV American Bible Society 1966, 1971, 1976 (includes the 4th edition of the New Testament). Used by permission.

Concordia Publishing House, St. Louis, Missouri
Copyright © 1979 Concordia Publishing House
MANUFACTURED IN THE UNITED STATES OF AMERICA

Library of Congress Cataloging in Publication Data

Weisheit, Eldon.
　　The Gospel for kids, series C.

　　1. Children's sermons.　　I. Title.
BV4315.W3734　　　　　252'.53　　　　　79-9730
ISBN 0-570-03278-4

Preface

This is my eighth preface for a book of children's sermons. The last six were written in as many years—a sermon a week for six years with a few extra for the possible bonus Sundays in Epiphany and Pentecost.

Perhaps I have nothing left to say in prefaces. The previous seven seem to be mini-courses about or sales pitches for special sermons for children in the Sunday morning worship service. The fact that the series lasted for six years indicates the instruction and persuasion are no longer necessary.

But I still have many children's sermons to go. I started preparing sermons, not for print, but for the kids in Trinity Lutheran Church, McComb, Mississippi, 17 years ago. I now am preparing them for the kids at Fountain of Life Lutheran Church, Tucson, Arizona.

During those years of preaching children's sermons I have appreciated the help and encouragement that others have given me. I hope that those sermons of mine that made it into print have also been of help to others.

The real blessing of those 17 years of preparing, preaching, and publishing children's sermons has been in my own spiritual life. The weekly study of a portion of God's word and the application to children in simple, uncluttered language, has given the Holy Spirit a chance to speak clearly to me. I thank Him for letting me know Jesus Christ and for letting me share in His ministry on earth.

Eldon Weisheit

Scripture Index

The children's sermons in this book are based on portions of the Gospel selections of the Three-Year Lectionary Series C.

Matthew			
2:11	25	13:35b	47
Luke		14:12-14	101
1:45	15	14:27-29	103
2:10, 11	17	15:1, 2	105
2:21	21	15:11, 12, 23, 24	51
2:28-30	19	16:13	107
3:6	11	16:29-31	109
3:15, 16	13	17:1	111
3:21, 22	27	17:17, 18	113
4:13	45	18:6-8a	115
4:21	31	18:14b	117
4:25, 26	33	19:3, 4	119
5:8	35	19:13	125
6:20, 21	37	19:38-40	55
6:31	39	20:9, 13, 14	53
6:39	41	20:37, 38	121
7:8	75	21:9, 18, 19	123
7:14, 15	77	21:28	9
7:41, 42	79	23:38, 42	127
9:23	81	24:6-8	57
9:30, 31	43	John	
9:62	83	1:1, 2, 14a	23
10:16	85	2:3-5	29
10:29	87	10:29, 30	63
10:41, 42	89	13:34	65
11:2-4	91	14:26	67
12:15	93	15:26b, 27	71
12:34	95	16:15	73
12:51	97	17:20, 21	69
13:4-5	49	20:30, 31	59
13:24	99	21:12	61

Contents

Know When to Stand Up	9
Don't Hide the Savior	11
Get Your Hopes Up	13
Happiness Is Believing	15
Don't Be Afraid! Why Not?	17
You Can Accept the Invitation Now	19
What Will You Take into the New Year?	21
The Gift You've Always Had	23
Watch What Others Do	25
One Hand Washes the Other	27
The Right Time Will Come	29
When the Words Come True	31
The Miracle That Includes Everyone	33
Don't Go Away, Jesus!	35
Look for Happiness That Will Last	37
A Ruler Is Used to Measure	39
When to Lead, When to Follow	41
Listen in on God's Conversations	43
Everyone Has a Weakness	45
When Will I See You Again?	47
Look Whose Name Is in the Paper!	49
You Can Come Home and Stay Home	51
Do You Hide from God?	53
Worship That Can't Be Stopped	55
Remember What You Already Have	57
Writing Is for Reading—and Doing	59
If You Have to Ask, It's Too Late	61
God's Greatest Treasure	63
A New Way to Live	65
So You Won't Forget	67
How Many Are One?	69
Talk About What You Have Seen	71

Know Who the Gift Is From	73
Jesus Tells You What to Do Because . . .	75
The Funeral That Didn't Last	77
To Give, You Must First Receive	79
Forget Yourself to Find the Way	81
Keep Your Eyes on Jesus	83
How Does God Talk to You?	85
Ask the Right Question	87
You Have a Choice	89
God's Catalog	91
Don't Be Fooled by Money	93
Know Where Your Heart Is	95
Move to Where the Peace Is	97
Know Who Will Open the Door	99
Give to Those Who Can't Give	101
Plan to Finish the Job	103
Praise or Blame for Jesus	105
But You Can Serve One	107
What Gets Your Attention?	109
Don't Spread Your Sin Around	111
When You Get What You Want	113
Knock—Again and Again	115
Which Name Tag Will You Wear?	117
Play Show-and-Go-Seek	119
He Is the God of the Living	121
You Are Safe with Jesus	123
What God Wants You to Do	125
The King Who Was Here Will Come Back	127

DEDICATED TO:
>   My brother: Wayne
>   My sisters: Wilma Ziller
>   Deanna Burris
>   And in memory of my brother:
>   Kenneth (1939—78)

Know When to Stand Up

The Word
Jesus said, "When these things begin to happen, stand up and raise your heads, because your salvation is near." Luke 21:28 (From the Gospel for the First Sunday in Advent)

The World
Any item that a child would buy as a Christmas present, a chair, or other seat.

Now is the time to start Christmas shopping. Suppose you were in a crowded store and decided you wanted to buy this (the gift) for your Mother. You would take it to the cashier. But the clerk is busy talking to another customer about size and color—the kind of things people talk about when they buy something. As you wait, you get tired. So you sit down. (Do it.) You look around at other people—then back to the salesperson. Now he is waiting on another customer. Because you sat down, you lost your place in line. Now you have to wait again. But this time you stand near the cashier. You want to be there when your time comes.

In our Bible reading Jesus tells us to stand up and hold our head up so we can see what is going on. He is not worried that we will lose our place in line when we are Christmas shopping. Instead He is thinking about the real gift of Christmas—the gift of salvation. He came to earth to be the Savior of all people. He is going to come back again to take us to be in heaven with Him. He does not want us to lose the gift that He died to give us.

But many people were not ready for Him when He came the first time. They did not believe He was the Messiah that had been promised in the Old Testament even though all the signs proved He was. Jesus knows that many people will not be ready for Him when He comes again. Many will be busy with other things. Many will have gotten tired of waiting. Some say they don't believe He is going to come anyway.

But Jesus says, "When these things begin to happen, stand up and raise your heads, because your salvation is near." The "things" he is talking about are the signs of trouble—strange events in the sky, people being afraid, bad weather. All of those and other things make us realize that we have to depend on God. They are signs to tell us that Jesus is coming again. Just as He came before, when He was born on the first Christmas, He will come again to take those who believe in Him to heaven.

He wants us to know that He is coming. He does not want us to lose interest and sit down. He doesn't want us to be so busy with other things that we are not ready for Him. Each time you hear the things that often scare us, the things about wars and storms, sickness and death, money problems and family worries; let each of them be a sign for you. They are signs that say, "Stand up and raise your heads, because your salvation is near."

Jesus is coming. He is ready to receive you. Be ready to meet Him.

Don't Hide the Savior

The Word
Jesus quoted the Old Testament Prophet Isaiah, who wrote, "All mankind will see God's salvation!" Luke 3:6 (From the Gospel for the Second Sunday in Advent)

The World
An Advent Wreath (or Christmas decoration) that can easily be moved around.

Many people use an Advent wreath like this to remind themselves that Jesus is coming. Since today is the Second Sunday in Advent, we would light two candles. Then next week the third; then the fourth as Christmas comes very near.

But where should I put the Advent wreath? I could put it here (under a chair or pew). But then it is hidden, and no one could see it. Or I could put it here (on the floor at the side of the room). It's not hidden here, but it's not in plain view either. Only a few people would see it. The best place to put the Advent wreath is right here, (on the altar or other obvious place). Then everyone can see it. The two lighted candles will remind everyone that Christmas is coming soon.

In our Bible reading Jesus quotes an Old Testament prophet who told us some things about the first Christmas when Jesus was to be born. Among other things, Isaiah wrote, "All mankind will see God's salvation." Jesus is God's way of saving the world. He came to die for everyone's sins. So part of His work is not only to pay for our sins but also to do it so everyone can see Him as Savior.

Our celebration of Christmas 1,900 years after He was born shows that the prophet was right. We are saying today that we see God's salvation for all people because Jesus is our Savior. So it is important that we see Jesus as the Savior in all our Christmas celebration. And it is important that we show Him to others.

Where will Jesus be in your Christmas celebration? Will He be hidden behind all the presents and decorations; so you forget about Him and others don't see Him as a part of your Christmas? That would be like hiding the Advent wreath under the pew. We can't have a Christmas with a hidden Savior.

Or will Jesus be over in the corner by Himself? Will you keep Jesus just for the Christmas Eve service or maybe a family devotion? That would be treating Him very much like the Advent wreath I put on the floor. Few people would see Jesus in your Christmas celebration.

Instead put Jesus out in the front and center—like the wreath on the altar. Let Jesus be a part of your parties—and your gifts. Let Him be a part of the shopping and the mailing. Because Jesus is your Savior, you can smile and not only say, "Merry Christmas," but you can give a merry Christmas to others when you show them their salvation.

Get Your Hopes Up

The Word

People's hopes began to rise, and they began to wonder whether John perhaps might be the Messiah. So John said to all of them, "I baptize you with water, but someone is coming who is much greater than I am. I am not good enough even to untie His sandals. He will baptize you with the Holy Spirit and fire. Luke 3:15, 16 (From the Gospel for the Third Sunday in Advent)

The World

Two Christmas packages and an envelope containing an airline ticket.

Let me tell you a story about Greg. Greg was about your age. His family moved far away one summer. He liked his new home, but at Christmas he wanted to go back to where they used to live. His grandparents lived back there. He knew they would like for him to stay with them. But he wondered how he would get there. If only they would invite him. Maybe he would get some money for Christmas and could buy his own ticket. Greg's parents told him not to get his hopes up.

One day a package arrived from his grandparents. There was a gift for his father (show it) and one for his mother (show it). But for him—only this envelope. Then Greg thought: it is an invitation. Their gift to me is an invitation to stay with them. Now all he needed was an airline ticket. His hopes were up. On Christmas he opened the envelope. Look—it is a ticket. He could fly home on vacation.

Greg had his hopes up because he thought he had an invitation. But he received more than he had hoped for. That happened to the Jewish people long ago. When John the Baptist came and preached, many people got their hopes up. They hoped he was the Messiah—the Savior their people had been expecting for many years. But John told the people not to get excited about him. Someone much greater was coming. If they got their hopes up over John, what would be their joy when they heard Jesus! Jesus was coming to be God living with them. He would fulfill all the promises made in the Old Testament and give them salvation. Through His work the Holy Spirit would come to give them a new life.

As Christmas comes nearer, we also get our hopes up—hopes for presents and parties, vacation and fun. Plan to have a good time at Christmas. But as you get your hopes up about the celebration of Christmas, remember the stories about Greg and John the Baptist. Christmas offers more than presents and parties. Christmas offers God to you. When Christ was born, God came to be a part of our lives. What He offers is far greater than any other gift we could receive. The celebration we will have with Him will be far greater than any party we could have here.

Get your hopes up! Jesus is coming!

Happiness Is Believing

The Word

Elizabeth said to Mary, "How happy you are to believe that the Lord's message to you will come true!" Luke 1:45 (From the Gospel for the Fourth Sunday in Advent)

The World

A child's bow and arrow set wrapped (in a way that does not conceal its identity) as a Christmas gift.

Waiting for Christmas makes some people unhappy. They worry about what they will get for Christmas—especially if they want one special gift very much. Suppose, for example, that you wanted a bow and arrow set for Christmas. You have talked about the bow and arrows with your friends. You have even invited other kids over to play with your bow and arrow after Christmas. Then you wonder: What if I don't get the present I want? That could be a problem.

Then you see this package under the tree. And it has your name on it. You can't see what is in the package. But look at it's size and shape. Feel the long curved stick and the short sticks with points on them. Now you don't have to worry any more. You are already happy even before you open the package because you know what is in it.

We also want a Savior for Christmas—One who will change our lives each day to make us be what God wants us to be. We need Him to forgive our sins and to help us enjoy the life we have. Sometimes people worry about the gift of the Savior. They wonder: Is Jesus really the Savior? Can He take away all our sins? Can He be with us today? Can He take us to heaven?

In our Bible reading, Mary, who was to become the mother

of Jesus, and her cousin Elizabeth talk about the baby before He was born. Elizabeth says, "How happy you are to believe that the Lord's message to you will come true." Elizabeth could see that Mary was already happy. Mary believed what God had told her. Even though Jesus was not yet born, she knew that she had a Savior. She did not have to wait until the day of His birth to be happy about knowing Jesus.

We also can be happy because we believe in Jesus. We do not have to wait until He comes on Judgment Day to know that He is the one who saved us. Even though we have not seen Him, we can see what He has done. Like the wrapped gift, He has already been given for us. Because you already know about Jesus, people can say to you, "How happy you are to believe that the Lord's message to you will come true!"

Don't Be Afraid! Why Not?

The Word

But the angel said to them [the shepherds], "Don't be afraid! I am here with good news for you, which will bring great joy to all the people. This very day in David's town your Savior was born—Christ the Lord!" Luke 2:10, 11 (From the Gospel for Christmas Day)

The World

A business envelope with "DON'T BE AFRAID!" written on the outside and message (see below) on the inside.

Our Bible reading tells us that an angel came to some shepherds. The angel said, "Don't be afraid!" I can imagine the shepherds thought or said, "Why not?"

The shepherds had reasons to be afraid. They were not used to talking to angels. They did not know what the angel would tell them. They knew angels came from God and God was holy. The shepherds might have been afraid that the angels would remind them of all the wrong things they had done. But the angel said, "Don't be afraid!"

To understand how the shepherds may have felt, let's imagine that you broke a large window in a store. The store owner said he would send you the bill. You don't have much money, and you know that big windows cost a lot. One day you get this letter from the store. You are afraid to open it. But look what it says on the outside—"Don't Be Afraid!"

So you open the letter. There is no bill. Instead there is a letter. It says, "I forgive you for breaking my window. I repaired it myself. You don't owe me anything." Then you aren't afraid anymore. But what would have happened if you had been afraid to open the envelope? Then you would never have received the good news that the bill was paid.

The shepherds did not run away from the angel. They stayed to listen for the reason why they didn't have to be afraid. The angel said, "I am here with good news for you, which will bring great joy to all the people. This very day in David's town your Savior was born—Christ the Lord!"

The shepherds did not have to be afraid of God. God had come to live with them. He came as a Savior to forgive their sin and to stay with them.

The Christmas message for us is: "Don't be afraid!" Don't be afraid because you have done wrong. Don't be afraid because you or someone you know is sick. Don't be afraid because you have problems at school or home. Don't be afraid of accidents and storms.

You may ask, Why not? Why shouldn't I be afraid? The angel answers, "You have a Savior, Christ the Lord." The Savior loves you. He tells you God is always on your side. You may still have problems and worries. But God is with you. Don't be afraid!

You Can Accept the Invitation Now

The Word

Simeon took the child in his arms and gave thanks to God: "Now, Lord, You have kept Your promise, and You may let Your servant go in peace. With my own eyes I have seen Your salvation." Luke 2:28-30 (From the Gospel for the First Sunday After Christmas)

The World

A pair of roller (or ice) skates in a box.

Imagine that several days before Christmas a friend invited you to a rollerskating party during the holidays. The friend said you had to bring your own skates. You'd like to go to the party. All of your friends will be there. But you have no skates.

Yet your mother tells you to accept the invitation. She tells you not to worry about the skates. Then you realize that one of the packages under the Christmas tree might be a pair of rollerskates for you. So you accept the invitation.

On Christmas morning, you open this package—sure enough, a pair of skates. You had already accepted the invitation to the party because you believed the box had skates for you. And what you believed was right. You are going to the party.

Something like that happened to an old man named Simeon in our Bible reading. God had told him he would not die until he saw the Messiah. For years the Jewish people had been waiting for the Messiah to come. They knew He would be their Savior. But many of the people had given up hope. They thought the Messiah would never come. Yet Simeon knew the Messiah would come soon; because he was an old man ready to die.

One day Simeon saw Joseph and Mary bring the Baby Jesus to the temple. The Holy Spirit told Simeon that the Baby was the Messiah. Simeon said, "Now, Lord, You have kept Your promise, and You may let Your servant go in peace. With my own eyes I have seen Your salvation." Simeon already knew he had a Savior because he believed God. He was like you when you believed you had skates even before you opened the package. Yet Simeon rejoiced when he saw the Baby. The promised gift was his. With his own eyes he saw God's gift to him.

You also live with a promise from God. He has promised you that He will take you to heaven because Jesus has died for you and has risen from the dead. Even though you have not yet seen Him with your eyes, you can accept His invitation. You know Jesus is coming to take you home with Him forever. When He does come, He will not be a stranger. God has promised that He would come. We already live as though He were here.

Remember the old man Simeon and realize how you are like him. God told Simeon, and He tells you, that a Savior is coming. Believe that promise. And when you see the Savior your eyes also will see God's salvation.

What Will You Take into the New Year?

The Word
A week later, when the time came for the baby to be circumcised, He was named Jesus, the name which the angel had given Him before He had been conceived. Luke 2:21 (The Gospel for the Circumcision and the Name of Jesus)

The World
A calendar (showing signs of use) for the year just closed and another (fresh and new) for the year just started.

Look at this calendar for last year and think of what you did in 19__. You had many happy days last year. Last year's vacation, parties, and other good times are also represented by days on this calendar. Other days were good because you learned something that would help you the rest of your life.

You want to take the good things you have learned and the memories of the happy days with you into the new year. Those things will become a part of this calendar for the year 19__. Aren't you glad we don't start every year in a completely new way, without any contact with the past? If we did, we'd lose all the good things from the years past. Think of all the things you want to take with you into the new year.

But there are other things you'd rather not take with you into the new year. Some of the days in the old year were bad. You did some things last year that you are ashamed of now and would rather forget. You wouldn't want them written down to spoil the new calendar. On other days you were disappointed and hurt. You may have picked up bad habits that will cause you troubles as long as you keep them. Wouldn't it be great if you could get rid of all the bad things when you start a new year? How great to start with a fresh, clean calendar!

Now you see the problem. We want to start the new year by taking all the good things from the past with us. But we also want to leave all the bad behind. But we can't always divide the two because each one is a part of our lives. That's why it is good to celebrate New Year's Day on the day Jesus was circumcised and named. Jesus helps us leave behind in the old year those things that hurt us and take those things into the new year that help us.

When Jesus came, He brought a new life to earth—a life that He would share with all people. He is our chance for a fresh start. But Jesus did not ignore the old life that was here. He came to save sinners—not to destroy sinners and start over.

The first thing we know about Him after His birth is that He was circumcised. The circumcision made a mark on His body to show that He obeyed the Law. He knows about our sins. He obeyed the Law in our place so we can be forgiven. As we start the new year, we take His love and forgiveness with us into 19.... We do not have to be afraid of the past, because Jesus has taken the problems for us. We can be happy about the future, because Jesus goes with us into the new year.

The Gift You've Always Had

The Word

Before the world was created, the Word already existed; He was with God, and He was the same as God. From the very beginning the Word was with God. . . . The Word became a human being and, full of grace and truth, lived among us. John 1:1, 2, 14a (From the Gospel for the Second Sunday After Christmas)

The World

A child's tea set with the teapot still wrapped in packing material in a box.

You've had time to look at, use, and even lose, some of your Christmas presents by now. Suppose one of your gifts this year was this box with cups and saucers. They are pretty—the kind of gift you should take care of. Perhaps you have already thanked the person who gave them to you. Now is the time to put them away carefully so they will not be broken.

It would be a good idea to put them back in the box they came in. Here it is. As you go to put the cups and saucers back in the box, you discover there is something else in the box. Look (show the teapot). You had missed part of the gift. When you opened the package, you had found part of the gift, but the most important part was hidden in the packing material. The teapot was yours before. But you didn't know it. Because you hadn't found it, you almost threw it away.

In some ways the people who lived at the time of Jesus' birth treated their gift from God like this tea set. They knew God had given them many great gifts. He had created the world. He had given them food and clothing. He had freed their ancestors from slavery. He had given them a land of their own. They appreciated all of those gifts—just like you may have appreciated these cups and saucers.

But they almost missed the most important part of the gift from God. Our Bible reading tells us: "Before the world was created, the Word already existed; He was with God, and He was the same as God. From the very beginning the Word was with God. The Word became a human being and, full of grace and truth, lived among us."

The Word is Jesus, our Savior. He always existed—just like the teapot was always in the box. But the people did not know about Him. They accepted and appreciated the other gifts from God. But they didn't see the most important of all. Then He was born. He became a person to live with us. He was filled with God's grace. He brought us God's truth.

But some people did not see the great gift of God. Some did not find Jesus because they saw only the other gifts. Christmas is past for this year. You received many gifts. You had good times. You enjoyed your vacation. All that is good. God wants you to have a good life.

But God also wants your good life to last forever. He has given you a Savior to forgive your sin. He gave His life for yours. Don't miss the most important part of God's Christmas gift to you. As you are putting the other gifts away, think about God's love for you in Christ. Keep that part of your gift with you every day.

Watch What Others Do

The Word
They [some men who came from the East] went into the house, and when they saw the Child with His mother Mary, they knelt down and worshiped Him. Matthew 2:11 (From the Gospel for Epiphany)

The World
A food tray, eating utensils, napkins.

When I go through a new cafeteria line I always feel confused. Maybe you've been in a cafeteria line at school or camp. Or if you've eaten dinner with your family in a cafeteria where you have to pick up your own tray and food, you know what I mean. First, you have to find the tray. Then you have to know if you need to take a knife, fork, and spoon. Sometimes you don't need all of them, and sometimes they are already on the table. Then you have to find the napkins. After you finally get your food to the table, you have to decide if you leave the food on the tray as you eat it, or if you put the various dishes on the table and take the tray back.

But there's an easy way to handle a new cafeteria line. Do what I do. Watch the people in front of you. If they seem to know what they are doing, you do the same thing. That way you'll find everything you need, and all will work out fine.

And I'll tell you someone else to watch so you know what to do. Watch the men in our Bible story for today who came from a far away land when Jesus was born. Remember the story—they followed the star until they came to Bethlehem. Then they went into the house where Jesus was.

Would you have known what to do if you had been there? Sometimes we don't know what to do when we are with Jesus.

We know many things about Him. We know He died to pay for our sins. That He rose from the dead three days later. He also tells us He is still with us. In fact, He promised to be with us until the end of the world.

But what do we do when we are with a Savior like that? We don't want to ignore Him. If you want to know what to do, watch what those men did who followed the star. The Bible says, "When they saw the Child with His mother Mary, they knelt down and worshiped Him."

When they saw Jesus, they knew He was the Son of God. So they did the only thing you can do with God. They worshiped Him. The same thing happened many times in the life of Jesus. Often when people first met Him they didn't know who He was. But when they saw His power and felt His love, they knew He was God. And they worshiped Him.

You can follow their example and worship Him today. People have been worshiping Him for all those years since the shepherds and wise men first worshiped Him at His birth. Not all people worship Him. Some have not yet recognized that He is God. We don't want to follow them. Instead we want to follow those who have seen the love of God in Jesus Christ. We worship Him as our Savior. Others who see us at worship will know that He is the Savior too.

One Hand Washes the Other

The Word
After all the people had been baptized, Jesus also was baptized. While He was praying, heaven was opened, and the Holy Spirit came down upon Him in bodily form like a dove. And a voice came from heaven, "You are My own dear Son. I am pleased with You." Luke 3:21, 22 (From the Gospel for the First Sunday After the Epiphany)

The World
An ashtray filled with ashes, a wastebasket, a bowl of water, soap, and towel.

When you have one dirty hand, you have a problem. (Dump the ashes into one hand and close the hand. Drop the ashes into the wastebasket.) See—this hand is dirty. I wouldn't want to eat with it. I wouldn't want to brush my teeth or change clothes. The other hand is clean. If it's time for dinner, someone would say, "Go wash your hands."

So you get some water and soap. (Do it). Now look what happens. Even though one hand is clean and only one dirty, you wash both. (Do it.) You need the clean hand to wash the dirty one. As you use the soap, the dirt from the dirty hand goes onto the clean hand. But when you rinse them off, both are clean. (Dry the hands.) There is an old saying, "One hand washes the other." Now both are clean.

God has two kinds of children. He has us who are sinners— we are like the dirty hand. And He has Jesus, His holy Son, who is like the clean hand. God sees the sins of the world and says, "You must be washed clean." The clean Son of God joins the dirty children of God, and together they are cleaned—like one hand washing the other.

We hear about our being made clean in the Bible reading for

today. People were coming to be baptized—like we are baptized. They wanted their sins washed away. But water alone will not take away sin. So Jesus came to be baptized too. He added a new meaning to the washing of baptism. He had no sin, but He shared in the sin of the rest of us. He let us put our dirt on Him. Then He died on the cross and rinsed all the dirt away.

We needed to be baptized because we are sinners. Jesus was not baptized because He was a sinner, but because He wanted to help make us clean.

Think of your baptism each time you use one hand to wash the other. Remember that your baptism is still a part of your life. Each day you are made clean again because Jesus still lives with you. He is still the holy Son of God. And in your baptism He gave that holiness to you.

The Right Time Will Come

The Word
When the wine had given out, Jesus' mother said to Him, "They are out of wine." "You must not tell Me what to do," Jesus replied. "My time has not yet come." Jesus' mother then told the servants, "Do whatever He tells you." John 2:3-5 (From the Gospel for the Second Sunday After the Epiphany)

The World
A piece of raw bread dough and a baked roll.

Are you hungry when you come home from school? Suppose you said, "I'm hungry! What's to eat?" Your mother might say, "I'm baking rolls. You'll have to wait."

But you keep telling her how hungry you are and that you've got to eat. Finally, she might say, "Okay, here's your roll now, (show the raw dough). Go ahead and eat it." But you know this won't taste good. If you would have waited until your mother was ready to feed you, you would have received this. (Show baked roll.) And this tastes good.

In our Bible reading for today Jesus' mother asked Him for help. She was helping the family at a wedding, and they ran out of wine. She told Jesus about the problem. Jesus said, "My time has not yet come." He did not help His mother the moment she asked. But she knew that the time would come when He would help. We know she believed He would do what she asked because she told the servants to wait for His help. Later Jesus told the servants to put water into jars, and the water became wine.

Turning water into wine was Jesus' first miracle. Jesus shows not only that He can do miracles and that He will help, but also that He gives His help at the time we need it the most.

When we ask God for help, we often want Him to give it right now. Sometimes we don't see what God had already done to help us. And we often do not see the other help that we have from Him. We just want what we ask for, and we want it right then.

But Jesus does not want to give us the raw dough; He wants us to wait for the blessings He has prepared for us. They will be the best.

Sometimes we don't understand why Jesus does not answer our prayers the moment we ask. But remember—because He has the power to do miracles He also has the ability to know what is best for us. He knows that many people want the miracles of good health, good grades, victories at ball games, and new bicycles. But sometimes we do not see that we need the big miracles of forgiveness of sins and eternal life. If we only ask for the things we need now, we are forgetting that Jesus has given His life so we can see the greater gift of His love and forgiveness for us.

When you pray, do not be afraid to ask Jesus to help you in any way you want. But remember that if He tells you to wait a while. He is answering your prayer. His time will come to help you. Because He loves you, He wants you to wait until the right time to receive what you asked for.

When the Words Come True

The Word
[Jesus said to them]: "This passage of Scripture has come true today, as you heard it being read." Luke 4:21 (From the Gospel for the Third Sunday After the Epiphany)

The World
A package of cookie mix and some baked cookies (if practical a cookie for each child present).

One time Jesus went back to His hometown Nazareth. When He went to worship with His family and friends, the leaders of the synagog asked Him to read from the Bible. Jesus read from the prophet Isaiah. The reading said that someone would come to help the people. The One who was to come would bring good news to the poor. He would free the captives and the oppressed and heal the blind and save the people.

After Jesus finished the reading He said, "This passage of Scripture has come true today, as you heard it being read." The words were true because Jesus was there. He came to do the things Isaiah had promised. He came to save the people.

The words of the prophet came true on that day—but not only on that day. They also come true for us today. Each time we hear the story that tells us about Jesus, the words come true again. We hear the message of His birth, death, and resurrection from the dead often. Each time we hear about what Jesus has done for us, the promises of the Bible come true again. Today the Good News is preached to us. Today we are made free. Today we are saved.

To show you how the same words can come true again and again, I want to read you something else. (Read part of the instructions from the cookie mix. Include the part that tells how many cookies it will make.) Those words were written and printed a long way from here. The words tell us about cookies. But there are no cookies until someone reads the words and follows them to make the cookies. The words come true, and cookies are made each time someone reads and follows the instructions. They come true over and over again in many places—each time someone makes cookies.

The words that Isaiah wrote and Jesus read have also been printed over and over again. Today many people will hear those words. Every day people hear the message of Christ who came as the Savior of the world. The words are not just letters in a book. Just like the words on the package of cookie mix, they are words that tell us what will happen. When we read the words and follow them, the things they talk about happen again.

Like the instructions for baking cookies, the words of Jesus are to be followed. We follow His words by believing Him, by knowing that He came to be our Savior. The things He talked about and did long ago, happen again today. Today God loves you. Today you are saved.

The Miracle That Includes Everyone

The Word

Jesus said, "Listen to me: it is true that there were many widows in Israel during the time of Elijah, when there was no rain for three and a half years and a severe famine spread throughout the whole land. Yet Elijah was not sent to anyone in Israel, but only to a widow living in Zarephath, in the territory of Sidon." Luke 4:24, 26 (From the Gospel for the Fourth Sunday After the Epiphany)

The World

A bag of fruit. If practical a piece of fruit for each child. Or ask 10 children to come forward and have at least 12 pieces of fruit.

The Bible tells us about many miracles. Each miracle shows something about God. Miracles show that He loves people and helps us. They show His power, wisdom, and authority. But miracles can show different things depending on how one looks at them. In our Bible reading Jesus talks about miracles that God did through Elijah in the Old Testament. God provided food for a widow and her son. When the son died, God brought him back to life.

But Jesus reminded the people in Nazareth that there were other hungry widows back then. God did not help the others. Others had sons who died, but they were not brought back to life. The miracles for the widow were great, but what about the others? Miracles give answers to some. The woman knew God loved her. But the miracles gave questions to others. They asked, "Why doesn't God help us?"

You can see the problem by looking at this sack. What's in the sack? Something good, something bad, or nothing? It could contain garbage, food, or blank paper. We wonder about the sack, like we wonder about God. But I can give Jim an orange out of the sack. Now we all learned something about what was in the sack. It contained something good for Jim.

The miracles that came through Elijah were also good for the widow. They showed God's power and His love for her. The other people could see the miracles, or read about them, and they too would learn about God.

But the orange was not only for Jim. If I want all of you to know the sack has good things in it, then each of you should receive something. Here—the sack has an orange for all of you. And some left over. Now you know what was in the sack because you received something from it.

Jesus told the people He came to do something far greater than the miracles they saw Him do then, or the miracles they read about in the Old Testament. Those miracles helped only a few people. But Jesus came to give us the greatest of all miracles—one that would include everyone. He gave His life to pay for the sins of every person. He came to save not just one person, or a few people, or a family, or one city, or one country. He died for all.

Miracles still happen today. When they happen to us, we thank God. When they happen to others, we also thank God. But the greatest miracle is the one that happens to all of us. You are a part of that miracle today. You do not just hear about what happened long ago. Today God loves you. Today your sins are forgiven. Today Jesus Christ is with you.

Don't Go Away, Jesus!

The Word
When Simon Peter saw what had happened, he fell on his knees before Jesus and said, "Go away from me, Lord! I am a sinful man!" Luke 5:8 (From the Gospel for the Fifth Sunday After the Epiphany)

The World:
Two children about, but not exactly, the same height.

(Ask the two children to stand side by side. Then ask which one is taller. Discuss briefly the difference in their heights. Then ask the taller to stand beside yourself. Again ask which one is taller—you or the child. Explain that if the child wants to look tall, he would not stand by you but would stand by the other child.)

It makes no difference if you are tall or short. But it does make a difference if you are a sinner or not. Peter never thought of himself as being a bad sinner when he compared himself to the other fishermen who worked with him. He did some wrong things, but so did they.

Then one day Jesus went fishing with Peter and his crew. Even though they had caught nothing before, Jesus helped them catch the biggest load of fish Peter had ever seen. Peter then realized that Jesus was not an ordinary person. He knew that Jesus was also God. Then Peter also saw his own sin. When Peter compared himself to the other fisherman, he didn't think he was so bad. But when he compared himself to Jesus, he saw what a sinner he really was. So he said, "Go away from me, Lord. I am a sinful man!"

If we want to make ourselves look good, we can compare our behavior to other people's. We can always find someone who has done as much or more wrong than we have. But Jesus invites us to come and be with Him. When we stand by Him, we see how holy He is, and we are reminded of our own sins.

We don't like to be reminded of our sins. Sometimes we also feel like Peter and want to say, "Go away, Jesus. I'm too bad to be near You."

But Jesus didn't go away from Peter. And He won't go away from us. Instead He does something to help us. (Pick up the taller child so her head is even with your own.) I don't have to be taller than Cindy if I share my height with her by lifting her up. Jesus doesn't have to be more holy than we are if He shares His goodness with us.

Jesus has lifted us up by giving us His goodness. He does not want us to leave Him. Instead He wants us to stay near Him and to be comfortable with Him. When we think of our sin and remember how holy Jesus is, we can say, "Don't go away, Jesus! Stay with us and make us holy too."

Look for Happiness That Will Last

The Word

Jesus looked at His disciples and said, "Happy are you poor; the Kingdom of God is yours! Happy are you who are hungry now; you will be filled! Happy are you who weep now; you will laugh!" Luke 6:20, 21 (From the Gospel for the Sixth Sunday After the Epiphany)

The World

Two stacks of school papers (either from a child's workbook or duplicated material), two report cards, and a red marker pen.

Jesus says you should be glad if you are poor, hungry, and if you cry. That sounds strange, doesn't it? But remember—He's talking about now. He says if you are poor, hungry, and cry *now;* later you will be in the Kingdom of God; you will be filled; and you will laugh. Jesus does not want you to be unhappy. He does not want you to hurt. Jesus is thinking about all of your life both here on earth and in heaven. Sometimes you may think only about now. Jesus says it is better for you to think about your problems now; so you can be happy in the future.

Let's take this school work as an example. We'll say this stack belongs to Chris, and this stack belongs to Pat. On the first paper Chris gets a "Good." (Write this and other comments on the papers.) Pat gets an "F." On the second paper Chris gets "Excellent," but Pat gets a "You Can Do Better." Chris is happy. Pat is sad.

Chris doesn't study because he thinks he is doing fine. Pat studies hard because he is afraid he will fail. When the semester ends, the class has a big test. Chris gets a D-. The grade goes on his report card. (Do it.) Pat gets a B+. The good grade goes on his report card. Chris is sad. Pat is happy.

Because Chris thought he knew it all, he didn't study. Pat

knew he had to study, so he worked hard. Chris was happy, but ended up sad. Pat was sad, but ended up happy. Which do you think is better?

Jesus does not want us to hide from our sins and our problems now. We should not pretend that everything is okay. If we do, we will depend upon ourselves. Then when our lives end, we will be disappointed. But if we admit our sins and problems now, we will know we will need help. Then we can ask Jesus to forgive us and to help us. We can learn to depend on Him because He has been good in our place. We can admit our problems because we know He will help us. He gives us His life; so we do not have to rely on ourselves. Because He is with us, we will be happy when our life ends.

Jesus wants you to be happy even now. But He wants you to have the kind of happiness that will last forever. Even if you have sorrows and problems now, you can depend on Jesus to stay with you and to give you the happiness that will last forever.

A Ruler Is Used to Measure

The Word

Jesus said, "Do for others just what you want them to do for you." Luke 6:31 (From the Gospel for the Seventh Sunday After the Epiphany)

The World

A wooden yardstick.

A yardstick like this can be used for many things. I could use it as a stake to hold up a houseplant that wants to tip over. I could use it as a slat or rod to hold up a curtain. Or I could burn it to make a fire to roast hot dogs. (Let the children join in suggesting other uses for the yardstick.)

But what was the yardstick made for? The purpose of the yardstick is to measure things. It's to show how tall you are. Or how long a piece of string is. The yardstick may be used for many other things, but it was made to be used as a ruler to measure how long things are.

Our Bible reading for today is like a yardstick. We call it the Golden Rule. Jesus said, "Do for others just what you want them to do for you."

We can use the Golden Rule in many ways. Some people make signs and posters with these words. The Golden Rule is often printed on rulers and pencils. We also use the words as a memory verse. We can also use the Golden Rule to show that other people are wrong because they do not treat us the way we want to be treated.

But Jesus did not give us the Golden Rule to be used in those ways. The purpose of the Golden Rule is to help us know how to treat other people. By thinking about how we feel, we can know how others feel. The Golden Rule is a way to measure someone else's life by comparing it to our own, just as this yardstick measures a string when the two are held together.

When I know how I feel I can understand how others feel. When I am lonely, I like someone to talk to me. When I do something wrong, I want others to forgive me. If I were hungry, I would want someone to give me something to eat. If I were hurt, I would want someone to help me. If I didn't know the way to heaven, I would want someone to tell me. You can think of many other things about yourself that also are true about other people.

The Golden Rule helps us understand others. Jesus did not just tell us to follow the Golden Rule. He also used it for Himself. He knows what it is like for you to be afraid; so He promises to be with you always. He knows what it is to be tempted; so He gives you His power to fight against temptation. He understood how we feel because we sin and hurt ourselves and others. So He took the punishment of sin for us and gives us forgiveness. He knows what it is to be afraid of dying; so He died for us and gave us a new life that will last forever.

The Golden Rule is not just a clever statement or a nice motto for life. It is a way for us to live that will make our lives better and the lives of others better. It is a way we can live because we have Jesus as a Savior.

When to Lead, When to Follow

The Word
And Jesus told them this parable: "One blind man cannot lead another; if he does, both will fall into a ditch." Luke 6:39 (From the Gospel for the Eighth Sunday After the Epiphany)

The World
Two children, two blindfolds, several children's books, all the same size, with jackets that have been removed.

I have a job that I would like Diane and Gary do for me. See, the jackets have been removed from these books. Could you put them back on, please? (Let the children do it.)

That was simple, wasn't it? But let's see if they can do it again. This time I will blindfold them. (Do it.) Now I'll take the jackets off the books and see if they can put them back on. Do you think they can? Sure, they can put *a* jacket on *a* book, but because they cannot see, they cannot know if they have the right jacket on the right book. A person who cannot see cannot do this job.

But there is one way that a blind person could do the job. Diane, you take your blindfold off. Gary, leave yours on. Now Diane can do the job that I asked her to do. And Gary can too. Diane, you match the book and the cover and give them to Gary. Then he can put the jacket on the book. (Have them do it.) Even though Gary cannot see, he can do the job when someone who can see helps him.

In our Bible reading Jesus tells us that a blind person cannot lead a blind person. He wants us to know that we are blind in some ways. We cannot see the way to heaven by ourselves. Because we are sinners, we cannot always avoid doing wrong and always see the way to do right. By ourselves we are spiritually blind. We cannot help each other. The blind cannot lead the blind.

But Jesus knows the way to heaven. He came to live with us so He could lead us to heaven with Him. When He lived on earth, He did not sin—and He gives us the credit for His good life. He sees the way to avoid sin and to do good—and He leads us to do the same.

Jesus leads us by sending others who know Him to guide us. Sometimes we are like Gary. Someone who can see must lead us. It is important that we know when we need to be led. And we must also follow someone who knows Jesus to lead us. Someone who is as blind as we are cannot lead us.

At other times we are like Diane. When Jesus leads us, we see the way to live through Him. Then He can use us to lead others. We can help others see the Savior who has helped us.

Sometimes we lead. Sometimes we follow. But Jesus is always our leader, and we always follow Him. And we want to lead others, so they will follow Him too.

Listen in on God's Conversations

The Word
Suddenly two men were there talking with Him [Jesus]. They were Moses and Elijah, who appeared in heavenly glory and talked with Jesus about the way in which He would soon fulfill God's purpose by dying in Jerusalem. Luke 9:30, 31 (From the Gospel for the Last Sunday After the Epiphany)

The World
A portable TV set.

Have you ever tried to watch TV without the sound? (Turn the video on but not the audio.) Can you guess what the people are saying? (Switch to several channels. Suggest possible conversations.)

But as long as we have to guess what the people are talking about, we won't really know. (Turn up the volume.) But when we hear the dialog, then we know what the people are talking about. (Turn TV off.)

The Bible reading for today is from the story that tells how Jesus' appearance was changed. The disciples always saw Him as a person like themselves. But one day they saw Jesus with Moses and Elijah. Jesus looked different. They saw Him as we will see Him in heaven. Jesus and the two men from the Old Testament were talking to each other.

Can you guess what they were talking about? Were they talking about what was happening in heaven? or about when Judgment Day will come? or about how God created the world? We don't have to guess what they talked about. Our Bible reading says, "[They] talked with Jesus about the way in which He would soon fulfill God's purpose by dying in Jerusalem."

Moses and Elijah talked with Jesus about the things that

would happen in a short time. Jesus would be killed on a cross and would rise from His grave. Even before those things happened, Moses and Elijah knew about them; because they had also been saved by Jesus. They had believed the promise that He would come to take away their sins. They must have thanked Him for what He had done for them. They must have encouraged Him to put up with the suffering and pain, so He would die for the sins of the world.

I'm glad we don't have to guess what Jesus and the other two talked about at the Transfiguration. When we listen in on their conversation, we know how important it was that Jesus die for us. We know that He was willing to give Himself for us. He wanted to do it because He loves us.

God doesn't want us to have to guess what He has to say. We can listen in on all of His conversations. We often see what God does. We see His power in the sunrise and sunset. We see his beauty in flowers and people. We see His concern for us in fields of grain and fruit. We see His wisdom in the stars. But watching those things can be like seeing TV without the sound. Then we have to guess what they mean.

But God invites you to hear what He has to say. In the Bible He tells you of His plan of salvation for you. He tells you how He loves you and wants to be with you. Listen in on all of God's conversations.

Everyone Has a Weakness

The Word
When the devil finished tempting Jesus in every way, he left Him for a while. Luke 4:13 (From the Gospel for the First Sunday in Lent)

The World
A drinking glass, a piece of bread, a piece of plastic, a hammer, a dish of water, and a lighted candle.

Our Bible reading says, "The devil finished tempting Jesus in every way." The devil tried to make even Jesus do something wrong. And Satan used every way that he knew how to trick Jesus into sinning.

We know that the devil also tempts us. Today we want to talk about the ways that he tries to make us sin. His temptations are like threats to us. Some of his temptations may cause us to sin and others may not.

Suppose, for example, that I would threaten this glass with water. See—the water does not hurt it. (Pour some water into the glass and back into the container.) In fact, the water makes the glass clean. I can hold the glass over this flame, and it won't hurt the glass. (Do it.) If I held it there for a long time, the glass might break. But the glass can stand up under the flame for a while. But what would happen if I hit the glass with this hammer? (Do not do it, but show how you could.) That would break the glass. The glass is not afraid of water or fire, but the hammer would destroy it.

Now look at this piece of bread. The fire won't hurt the bread. In fact, it makes the bread into toast. The hammer would flatten the bread, but not destroy it. But what would happen if I dropped the bread into the water? That would ruin the bread. What a mess it would make!

Now look at this piece of plastic. The hammer and the water can't hurt it. But if I held it over this flame, it would melt, burn, and make a stink.

The glass, the bread, and the plastic can each be destroyed by one thing, but not even hurt by others. That's how you and I are about temptation. Some temptations don't bother us, but others do. Maybe you would never tell a lie or steal, but you might hate someone. You might never cheat in a ballgame, but you might cheat on a test at school.

Each of us have temptations that bother us; even though those same temptations might not bother some other people. We should know what sins are big problems for us; so we can ask Jesus for help. We can fight against temptations because He has been tempted in every way that we have. Yet He did not sin. Instead He paid for our sins so when we are tempted we can use His victory over sin to help us fight against those temptations.

We also need to understand that others may have trouble with temptations that do not bother us. Even if we had the chance, we would not do some sins. But others have trouble with that same sin. We need to understand that they have different temptations. We are not better than they are. Instead we need to show them the same help from Jesus.

Each of us has some weakness. But each one of us also has a great power in Jesus. He helps us fight temptation, and He forgives us when we sin.

When Will I See You Again?

The Word

Jesus said, "I assure you that You will not see Me until the time comes when you say, 'God bless Him who comes in the name of the Lord.'" Luke 13:35b (From the Gospel for the Second Sunday in Lent)

The World

An appointment book or calendar.

This is my appointment book. After someone visits my office, I sometimes say, "When will I see you again?" We talk about when we both have time; then we make an appointment to visit again.

You make appointments too. When you go to the dentist or doctor, the nurse will sometimes say, "When will we see you again?" Then she checks the appointment book and makes another date for you to come back.

Today we want to talk about your appointment with Jesus. You came here today to hear Jesus' word and to worship Him. See—here is your appointment for today. Jesus might say, "When will I see you again?" You might say, "Next Sunday." Then we'd mark your date with Jesus down in the book.

In our Bible reading Jesus was talking with some people who told Him to get out of town because King Herod wanted to kill Him. Jesus said He couldn't leave right away because He had appointments to help people. After He cured some people, He said He would leave. Then He added, "I assure You that you will not see me until the time comes when you say, 'God bless Him who comes in the name of the Lord.'" Jesus made an appointment to see the people again. When He came back to Jerusalem the next time, the people greeted Him in the streets by saying, "God bless Him who comes in the name of the Lord." We call that day Palm Sunday.

The night before Jesus died, He told the disciples that He would leave them. He said, "In a little while you will not see Me any more, and then a little while later you will see Me" (John 16:16). He made an appointment to come back to see the disciples even after He died. He kept that appointment when He rose from the dead.

Then Jesus made another appointment with His disciples. He said, "I will be with you always, to the end of the age" (Matthew 28:20b). Jesus kept that appointment when He sent the Holy Spirit to be with us and to make the life of Jesus a part of our lives. Jesus has made that same appointment with you. He did not say, "I'll see you next Sunday." Or ". . . the next time you come to church." He said He wants to be with you always.

Jesus puts His name on every page, every hour, of your appointment book. He wants you to be with Him always. Jesus puts His name on your appointment book. He comes to you. He also asks you to put your name on His appointment book. He also wants you to come to Him. He wants you to hear His word, to pray to Him, to share your life with Him.

Look Whose Name Is in the Paper!

The Word

Jesus asked, "What about those eighteen people in Siloam who were killed when the tower fell on them? Do you suppose this proves that they were worse than all the other people living in Jerusalem? No indeed! And I tell you that if you do not turn from your sins, you will all die as they did." Luke 13:4-5 (From the Gospel for the Third Sunday in Lent)

The World

Today's newspaper (from a large city) and a red marker pencil.

Do you read the Sunday paper? Not just the comic section, but the parts that tell you the news? If you do, look at the paper, and you will see that every day the paper has a story about someone dying. Look at this: (Show stories that tell of deaths and with the pencil write the number who died. If a tragedy has occurred in your area recently, mention it. Show the obituary page.)

In our Bible reading Jesus talks about something that would have been in the newspaper if there had been one in His day. Eighteen people were killed when a wall fell on them. Jesus asked, "Do you suppose this proves that they were worse than all the other people living in Jerusalem?"

Some people would answer Jesus' question, "Yes." Some think death is a punishment for sin. They see sickness, accidents, and other problems as signs of God's anger. If someone has a problem they ask, "I wonder what secret sin that person has done."

But Jesus answered His own question. He said, "No indeed!" The 18 people who were killed when the tower fell were not worse sinners than the others. God does not punish us for our sins by giving us sickness or causing us to die. Instead He sent His Son Jesus to die in our place. Because Jesus has died for us, our death will not destroy us. Our death will not be punishment because when we die He will take us to heaven.

But Jesus does want us to learn something from all the deaths we read about in the paper and from the 18 on whom the tower wall fell. He said, "If you do not turn from your sins, you will all die as they did."

The deaths of the 18 and all the deaths we see in this paper are reminders that we also will die sometime. Now is the time for us to turn from our sins and receive the forgiveness that Jesus offers us.

The newspaper only tells us about those who died or almost died. It does not list the millions of people who are not sick today, who have not had an accident, and who did not die. If God did punish sin by causing us to die, we would have to ask, "Why have millions of people continued to live day after day?" While rejoicing in His mercy, we could put out a newspaper that would give the names of all the people who are forgiven. It would include our names every day—even on the day we die.

You Can Come Home and Stay Home

The Word

Jesus went on to say, "There was once a man who had two sons. The younger one said to him, 'Father, give me my share of the property now.' So the man divided his property between his two sons." [The son left and was gone a long time. When he returned, the father said]: "'Go and get the prize calf and kill it, and let us celebrate with a feast. For this son of mine was dead, but now he is alive; he was lost, but now he has been found.'" Luke 15: 11, 12, 23, 24 (From the Gospel for the Fourth Sunday in Lent)

The World

Two doll figures, one labeled "Father," the other "Child," connected with a 2-foot red ribbon, a 2-foot green ribbon, a scissors.

This ribbon connects the father and child. In a story Jesus told, the son wanted to leave his father. He also wanted his inheritance, which he should not have received until the father died. So the son was saying that he wanted to pretend the father was dead. The father accepted the son's suggestion. He also pretended that the son had died. Later he said, "This son of mine was dead." They cut the ribbon between them. They were no longer connected.

Later the son realized he still loved and needed his father. He knew the father still loved him. So he went back home. The father said, "Now my son is alive. He was lost, but now he has been found. (Tie the green ribbon to each end of the red ribbon.)

Jesus tells us this story to show us that we can always come back to God. The father in the story is God. We are the son. When we tell God that we don't like the way He tells us to live, we cut our relationship with Him. We treat Him as though He were dead. We don't listen to Him, and we won't talk to Him. And we become dead to Him.

But our Father in heaven still loves us. He sent Jesus to bring us back to Him. Jesus came to share in our lives. He took our guilt. He became dead with us. So He is a part of us. Each of you can see Jesus tied to your life like this green ribbon is tied to the red ribbon connected with the child.

Jesus also rose from the dead and returned to the Father. He is still God; so He is also tied to the Father just as the green ribbon is also connected to the father.

If you feel separated from God, this story tells you that you can go back to Him. He wants you. He welcomes you back. He does not want you to be dead. He gives you a life that will last forever.

The story also tells you that you do not have to leave God. When you sin, you need not run away from God—Jesus forgives you and keeps you with your Father in heaven. When you have doubts or problems, you need not fall away from God. Instead you can stay with God and let Him help with the problem.

Remember the story of the son who came back to his father. Also remember that he stayed with his father from then on.

Do You Hide from God?

The Word

Then Jesus told the people this parable: "There was once a man who planted a vineyard, rented it out to tenants, and then left home for a long time. . . . Then the owner of the vineyard said, 'What shall I do? I will send my own dear son; surely they will respect him!' But when the tenants saw him, they said to one another, 'This is the owner's son. Let's kill him, and his property will be ours!'" Luke 20:9, 13, 14 (From the Gospel for the Fifth Sunday in Lent)

The World

A game appropriate for the children present.

In our Bible reading for today Jesus tells us why some people hide from God. Since we are here, we are not hiding from God now. But let's look at the Bible reading, so we won't hide from God later on in our lives.

Jesus tells the story of a farmer who rented his land out to tenants. The farmer left, and the tenants picked the grapes and sold them. But when the farmer sent his servant to collect his share of the profit, the tenants wouldn't divide. The farmer sent his son for the money. The tenants killed the son. The tenants knew the farm belonged to the farmer. But as long as he was gone, they could pretend it was theirs.

The same thing would happen if you owned this game. It's a fun game, so you would invite your friends over to play with you. Suppose one of your friends asked to borrow the game. So you would lend it to him. You would think that you could then go to his house and play your game with him. But he might not invite you. He might ask other friends to play with him. If he asked you to come to his house, his other friends would know that the game really belonged to you. He wants them to think the game belongs to him. So he doesn't invite you.

That seems unfair. And it is. But many people do the same thing to God. He has given us our lives and all that we have. He has given us family, friends, homes, health, and many other things. You would think that we would all want to share our lives with God because He has given us so much. And when we invite God to be with us, others know that what we call our own, directly or indirectly comes from Him. But some people want to pretend they have earned everything for themselves. So they hide from God.

But God still loves all people. He even sent His Son, Jesus, to earth. Jesus came to show us God's love and to help us see that God still wants to be with us. But a long time ago people killed Jesus; because they didn't want God around. Today many people ignore or deny Jesus. If they let Jesus be a part of their lives, they have to admit that He saves them.

Each of us should ask ourselves: Do I ever hide from God? Do I want people to think that I can pay for my own sins? that I can take care of myself? that I don't need God?

Remember how much God loves you. And how much He wants to be with you. Don't be afraid to show that you love God. Let others know that you depend on Jesus for your life now and your life forever.

Worship That Can't Be Stopped

The Word

[The disciples shouted]: "God bless the king who comes in the name of the Lord!" . . . Then some of the Pharisees in the crowd spoke to Jesus. "Teacher," they said, "command Your disciples to be quiet!" Jesus answered, "I tell you that if they keep quiet, the stones themselves will start shouting." Luke 19:38-40 (From the Gospel for the Sixth Sunday in Lent)

The World

A poster and a mailing tube (tube from paper towels will do) several inches shorter than the width of the poster.

If you wanted to mail this poster to a friend, you'd have to roll it up and put it in a mailing tube. (Push the poster through so it sticks out the other side.) But the postal clerk would tell you that you can't mail the poster with one end sticking out. So you shove it back. But then look what happens. If you solve the problem by pushing one side in, the other side sticks out. One end of the poster is always going to stick out.

Something like this happened on the first Palm Sunday. As Jesus came into the city, the people shouted, "God bless the king who comes in the name of the Lord! Peace in heaven and glory to God!" The people worshiped Jesus as though He were God. Some of the religious leaders who did not believe He was God became angry. They told Jesus, "Teacher, command Your disciples to be quiet!" They did not want other people to hear great things about Jesus. They were afraid that even more people would believe in Him. But Jesus said, "I tell you that if they keep quiet, the stones themselves will start shouting." The praise for Jesus was like the poster in this tube. It couldn't be hidden. The praise came from the disciples. But if the disciples had not shouted the message of Christ, someone else would have. Just as when I push one end of the poster in the tube, the other end comes out, if someone stops praising Christ, another will start. Because Jesus is God, He has to be praised. His glory and mercy cannot be hidden.

People have continued to praise Jesus for 1,900 years. Now it is our turn. We are the ones who can now see the great things that Christ does for us. Our worship shows that we believe He is not far away, but that He is present with us to receive our praise and to give us His blessings.

Jesus does not depend upon our praise, but we do depend upon His blessings. If we do not praise Him, someone else will. But those who worship Him are those who enjoy His presence, who share in His life because they know He has shared in theirs. Let your worship be the kind that can't be stopped. It's one of the things that you can do now—that you can also do forever.

Remember What You Already Have

The Word
[The angels said to the women]: "He is not here; He has been raised. Remember what He said to you while He was in Galilee: 'The Son of Man must be handed over to sinful men, be crucified, and three days later rise to life.'" Then the women remembered his words. Luke 24:6-8 (From the Gospel for Easter Sunday)

The World
A message (see below) on a folded piece of paper, five children's books with a picture or suitable gift stuck between the pages of one.

Jenny is going to help with the sermon today. First of all, will you hold this for me, Jenny. (Give her the folded paper.) Now, I have a gift for you. It is a picture of (describe the picture). The picture is in one of these books. I'll give it to you if you can tell me which book it is in and what pages it is between. Don't just take a guess. You have to name the right book and the right pages for the first time.

Don't give me your answer until you have thought about it. I gave you all the clues you need to know, which book and between what pages the picture is. Remember the clues I gave you. (Continue to give hints until the child remembers the paper.) Read the message out loud. "The picture is in (name of book) between page ___ and ___." Here is the picture.

Jenny had the answer all the time. But she had to remember what she already had. The same thing happened to the women who went to the tomb on the first Easter morning. Jesus had told them that He would die and rise again from the grave. But they had forgotten what He had said. They were sad that He died. Then they were scared that His body had been stolen. But the angels said, "Remember what He told you when He was in

Galilee: 'The Son of Man must be handed over to sinful men, be crucified, and three days later rise to life."

Then the women remembered. Their sadness and fear were gone. Jesus had said those things would happen, and they did. The women had His answer all the time just like Jenny had the answer on the paper she was holding.

Because Jesus rose from the dead a long time ago, you and I also have an answer now for many of the things that bother us. We are sad if someone we know dies. Sometimes we are afraid to think about the time we will die. Sometimes we feel guilty because we know we have done things wrong. Sometimes we are afraid that people will find out some of the things that we have done and we know we should not have done. Sometimes we think that God does not love us.

If you worry about those things, think about the message the angels spoke on Easter morning. "Remember what He said to you while He was in Galilee." Remember that Jesus told you He would die to forgive your sin. Remember that He said He loves you and will always be with you. Remember He said, "Because I live, you will live also."

Remember the message of Easter. It is a gift that you already have. Jesus has defeated death. He is alive. You already have the new life that He gives. Use it.

Writing Is for Reading—and Doing

The Word

In His disciples' presence Jesus performed many other miracles which are not written down in this book. But these have been written in order that you may believe that Jesus is the Messiah, the Son of God, and that through your faith in Him you may have life. John 20:30, 31 (From the Gospel for the Second Sunday of Easter)

The World

A sealed envelope (message below) and a food item from a nearby chain restaurant (or just the container).

Here is a letter. All of us like to get mail—especially when it has our name on it rather than "Occupant." So let's pretend your name is on this envelope. Would you pick up the letter, take it to your room, and leave it there? Of course, not. When you get a letter you open it. (Do it.) You are eager to read what it has to say. This letter says, "One of your friends has bought a treat for you. You can come get it at any time." And it is signed by (name the place of business).

That's a good letter. You would be glad to receive it and to read it. But you don't stop with reading it. You go get the treat. (Show it.) The letter was written for you to read it. After you read it, you wanted to receive what it offered.

Our Bible reading says that the Scripture is like this letter. It says, "But these have been written in order that you may believe that Jesus is the Messiah, the Son of God, and that through your faith in Him you may have life."

The gospels tell the life of Jesus. They are like a letter addressed to you; because Jesus came to live for you. So we don't take the Bible and put it on a shelf. It was written for us to read. So we read it.

When we read about Jesus, we learn that we are sinners. He tells us that we have done wrong. He also tells us that He suffered and died for us; so He has taken the blame for our sins. Then we read that He came back to life and that He still lives today. Today He gives us His love. Today He helps us.

After we've read what is written, we do it. John tells us that the Scripture was written to tell us about Christ so we could believe in Him and have eternal life. The message from God tells us that Jesus our Friend has a special treat for us. He has already paid for the treat. We receive it when we believe in Him. Our faith tells us we can repent and receive the forgiveness that He has earned for us. Our faith tells us we can ask Jesus to help us when we have problems. Our faith tells us that even when we die, we will live again.

Keep on reading the things that the Bible tells you about Jesus. Don't put His letter to you aside. When you read His message, also do it. Receive the gift He has for you every day.

If You Have to Ask, It's Too Late

The Word
Jesus said to them, "Come and eat." None of the disciples dared ask Him, "Who are you?" because they knew it was the Lord. John 21:12 (From the Gospel for the Third Sunday of Easter)

The World
A picture of someone whom the children would not recognize and a picture of Jesus.

Suppose this person (show picture of unknown person) came up to you and said, "Come to my house for dinner." It's nice to be invited to dinner. You might want to say, "Thank you, I'll be happy to come to dinner."

But where would you go to eat that dinner? Do you know who this is? It would be embarrassing to be invited to dinner by someone you did not know. You'd have to say either, "No, I can't come." Or, "Yes, I'd like to come, but you'll have to tell me who you are."

But what if this person (picture of Jesus) said to you, "Come and eat"? Do you know who it is? Would you know where to go to receive the dinner He offers you? Since you know who this is, you can accept the invitation. You know that Jesus is with you when you eat your meals at home or school. You know that God makes it possible for you to have food to eat, and Jesus comes to be with you so you can enjoy the meals with Him. I hope you speak a prayer before eating your meal and in that prayer you ask Jesus to be with you as you eat.

You can also accept the invitation from Jesus to come and eat by coming to church. God not only feeds your body, but He also gives you food and strength for your soul. Jesus calls

Himself the bread of life and says that if we receive Him we will not be hungry again. Today as you hear that Jesus loves you and forgives you, as you share worship with Him, you are accepting His invitation to come and eat.

Jesus wants you to know Him so you can hear His invitation and can accept it. If you do not know Him and listen to Him, you cannot receive what He has to offer. He shows us the importance of knowing Him in our Bible reading for today. After He died and rose again, His disciples went fishing. They caught no fish until Jesus appeared on the shore and told them where to drop their nets. Then with a net full of fish they went ashore and Jesus said, "Come and eat." The disciples knew who He was. Even though they had seen Him die on the cross and had watched Him be buried, they knew He was alive again and was standing in front of them. They accepted His invitation and ate breakfast with Jesus.

Jesus invites you to do many things. He invites you to accept His forgiveness and to forgive others. He invites you to ask Him for help. He invites you to live with Him now, and He invites you to go to heaven with Him forever. But for you to hear and accept His invitation, you must know who He is. He is the Savior who lives with us now. He speaks to us, and we hear Him. We know His voice and accept His invitations.

God's Greatest Treasure

The Word
Jesus said, "What My Father has given Me is greater than everything, and no one can snatch them away from the Father's care. The Father and I are one." John 10:29, 30 (From the Gospel for the Fourth Sunday of Easter)

The World
A piece of fruit, a child's toy, a piece of family jewelry, a child.

I've asked Susan to help me today. Let's pretend she is my daughter. I've brought some other things that are also mine. They are mine, but because Susan is my daughter, I have them for her. See—here is an apple. I hope you like that. Here is a toy for you, Susan. This is a necklace that came from my mother. If Susan were my daughter, someday I would give it to her.

Of all the things I have here, which one do you think I'd want to keep the most? I wouldn't mind losing the apple. I could get another one for Susan. I'd rather keep the toy, but it too could be replaced. How about the necklace? I can't get another one. Even if I could buy one like it, it would not be the one from my mother. You might think the necklace would be the most important thing I have here. But it isn't.

You all know what is the most important to me, don't you? Of course—it's Susan. A father would always feel his family is the most important thing he has. And your father in heaven feels the same way. In our Bible reading Jesus says, "What My Father has given Me is greater than everything, and no one can snatch them away from the Father's care."

God has made many wonderful things in this world. Think of the beautiful mountains and oceans, the rich fields that grow our food, the coal, oil, and other minerals in the ground. The beautiful flowers, music, the sun, and stars—all things—belong to God because He made them. But do you think those are the most important things that God has? No, they're not. The most important thing to God is you—you and all other people. God sent His own Son to suffer and die for you and all others. He wants you and all others to live with Him forever.

Some things in God's creation have already been destroyed. The Bible tells us that eventually all the world will be gone. But Jesus says nothing will ever take you away from God. People are the most important things God has.

God has given all people to Jesus because He died for all and rose from the dead. And Jesus reminds you that He and the Father are one. Since you belong to Jesus, you belong to God. We don't have to pretend we are His children, like I asked you to pretend that Susan was my daughter. We are the children of God, because Christ claimed us to be His. And nothing can take us away from God.

A New Way to Live

The Word

Jesus said: "And now I give you a new commandment: love one another. As I have loved you, so you must love one another." John 13:34 (From the Gospel for the Fifth Sunday of Easter)

The World

A small potted plant wrapped as a gift so no one would know what is in the package. Sign on the package: "Handle with Care. Perishable."

Notice the sign of this gift says, "Handle with care. Perishable." That sign means we have to take special care with this package. Can you think of some rules we should make so we take good care of the gift?

(Allow the child to help make a list of rules. Include: Don't drop. Don't shake. Don't squeeze. Don't put the package in a hot place. Don't put it in a cold place. Keep right side up. Don't let it get wet. Etc.)

We could keep adding more and more rules as long as we keep the gift wrapped. But let's open the gift. (Do it.) It's a plant. Now we know why the package had the warning on it. The plant needs to be watered and put in the right place. We know what the plant needs, so we don't need any extra rules.

Many times we treat each other like a package that is wrapped with a sign: "Handle with Care. Perishable." We make up all kinds of rules for how we should treat each other. Those rules never seem to help because we continue to hurt each other more and more. So often we make up more rules, and more rules. But the more rules we make, the more difficult it is for us to live together.

Jesus gave us a new way to live with one another. Instead of making up more rules, He tells us to take a good look at one another and to understand each other. Take the wrappings off so others know who we are. See through the wrappings that others use to hide behind, so you can know what people really need. Jesus gives us a way to live with one another after the wrappings are off. He says, "And now I give you a new commandment: love one another. As I have loved you, so you must love one another."

Each of us needs love from others. And all others need love from us. As long as we live in love, the kind of love that Jesus gave us, we don't need to keep making more and more rules. We will help each other because our love makes us want to help, not because a rule tells us we have to help. Sometimes we'd rather make more rules. We always want the rules to tell other people what they have to do. We are afraid to live by Jesus' new commandment, because we know that others will not always live by His rule of love. That's why Jesus tells us we are to love one another in the way He has loved us. Just loved us so much that He gave His life for us. By His love He shared in all of our wrong so we can share in all of His goodness.

When we feel that His commandment of love is not working, we don't solve the problem by making more rules. Instead, we see again the love that He is talking about. When we receive that love from Him, we can give it to others.

So You Won't Forget

The Word
Jesus said, "The Helper, the Holy Spirit, whom the Father will send in My name, will teach you everything and make you remember all that I have told you." John 14:26 (From the Gospel for the Sixth Sunday of Easter)

The World
The speaker's business cards or phone number on small pieces of paper (one for each child present, if practical).

Let's pretend that I am going to take all of you on a trip to (name a local shopping or recreational area). If I took you on the trip, I'd be responsible for you. So I want you to know my phone number. It is: _____. If you get lost, you can phone my home, and someone will take the message. Then I can find you.

Think of the good time we'd have on the trip. (Ask the children what they would like to do at the place you visit. Suggest different activities to show how the group could easily be divided.)

But if each of you wanted to do different things, we would all be separated. What would you do if it were time to go home and you couldn't find me? No problem. Remember, you are supposed to phone me. What is my phone number? (Let the children think about the number and talk about the difficulty of remembering a number one has heard only once.)

Instead of just telling you my phone number, I could have given you this. (Hand out the cards.) These cards have my phone number on them. When you have the card, you won't forget the number. All you have to do is to look at the card, and you could call me.

Jesus and His disciples had something like this happen to them. For three years Jesus had taught them many things. But the disciples didn't write down what He said. They thought He would always be with them. If they forgot something, they would ask Him to tell them again.

Then Jesus told the disciples He would be leaving them. They were afraid. They did not want to lose the good things He had taught them. But they wondered if they would forget all the things He had said and done.

Then Jesus said, "The Helper, the Holy Spirit, whom the Father will send in My name, will teach you everything and make you remember all that I have told you."

I gave you a card to help you remember my phone number. Jesus gave you something far better. His promise is not only for the disciples but also for us. Because the Holy Spirit helped the disciples, our faith does not have to depend upon how well these men remembered what Jesus did. The Holy Spirit guided those disciples as they preached about Jesus and as some of them wrote down the message of Jesus for us. Because the Holy Spirit was their helper, He is also ours. Through their work we know that Jesus is our Savior and that He lives with us today.

Your faith in Jesus today does not depend upon your memory. It depends on Jesus. And the Holy Spirit is your Helper. Just as my card helps you remember my phone number, the Holy Spirit uses the Bible so you do not forget Jesus and all He does for you.

How Many Are One?

The Word

Jesus said, "I pray not only for them, but also for those who believe in Me because of their message. I pray that they may all be one. Father! May they be in Us, just as You are in Me and I am in You. May they be one, so that the world will believe that You sent me." John 17:20, 21 (From the Gospel for the Seventh Sunday of Easter)

The World

A metal or plastic cookie container with a removable lid and two boxes of cookies.

How many things am I holding? (Hold the container in one hand, the lid in the other.) It's easy to see that I have two things. But (put the lid on the container) I still have the exact same things in my hands; though now I am holding only one thing—a cookie can. When the lid and the container are separated, they are two. When the lid is on the container, they are one.

In our Bible reading Jesus says He and the Father are one. We know God the Father and God the Son (hold the objects apart). But we also know there is only one God (put the lid on). Two become one.

But that's not all. Jesus says that all who believe in Him are also one with Him. There are lots of cookies in this box. (Pour the cookies into the container, and put the lid on.) But now all the cookies, the lid, and the container are one. This is one can of cookies. Jesus also wants us to be a single thing with Him and the Father. He says, "Father! May they be in Us, just as You are in Me and I am in You." When Jesus died for us, He took away the sins that separate us from God. We can go back to God and be one with Him. Jesus is the Savior who brought us back to

God. All who believe in Jesus as their Savior become at one with Him. Just as all the cookies in the container become one can of cookies, all of us in Christ become one people.

But that's not all. I still have another box of cookies that are not in the cookie can. And there are still other people who do not belong to Jesus because they do not believe in Him. I can put more cookies in with the others (do it), and more people can believe in Jesus if they hear about Him. Jesus prays for those who already believe and for those who will believe because they hear the message of those who already do.

Of course this container will hold only so many cookies, but Jesus has no limit on how many can believe in Him. He loves everyone and died for everyone. He says, "May they be one, so that the world will believe that You sent Me." Unless those of us who believe in Jesus show that we are at one not only with God but also with one another, the world will not believe that Jesus is the Savior. When we love one another, we show the world what Jesus has done for us—and we show what we want to do for them.

Then we can all be one in Jesus Christ.

Talk About What You Have Seen

The Word
Jesus said, "I will send Him (the Holy Spirit) to you from the Father, and He will speak about Me. And you, too, will speak about Me, because you have been with Me from the very beginning." John 15:26b, 27 (From the Gospel for Pentecost)

The World
A picture of Jesus, two large pictures showing actions that the child would be able to discuss.

What can you tell me about this picture? (Show one of the action pictures. Let the children talk about it. Help them make up a story or explain what is happening in the picture.)

Now let's talk about this picture. (Hold up the other picture but have it folded so the children cannot see it.) We can't talk about this picture, can we? (Let the children talk about not seeing the picture. Explain that they haven't seen it; so they can't talk about it.)

Now let's see what you can tell me about this picture. (Show the picture of Jesus.) What do you know about Him? (Let the children tell about His birth, miracles, death, resurrection.) You didn't see all of those things on this picture, but you knew about them because you know Jesus. Because you know Jesus, you can talk about Him.

In our Bible reading for today Jesus tells us how the Holy Spirit comes to us. He says, "I will send the Holy Spirit to you from the Father and He will speak about Me. And you, too, will speak about Me, because you have been with Me from the very beginning."

The Holy Spirit is God as a teacher. He comes to us to tell us about Jesus. He tells us that Jesus was born to share in our lives. He tells us that Jesus was God who became a person like us, He died for us, and He lives again. The Holy Spirit tells us that Jesus did all of these things for us.

Jesus tells us that because the Holy Spirit speaks to us about the Savior, we too can speak about Him. Because we have heard about Jesus, we can talk about Him. You could tell others about this picture, because you had seen it. But you could not tell others about this picture, because you had not seen it.

Today is Pentecost; we celebrate this day because the Holy Spirit came to those who followed Jesus; on the 50th day after Jesus' resurrection the Holy Spirit gathered the first group of believers in Jerusalem. We also celebrate the Holy Spirit's coming to us today so we can know about Jesus. And we also know that the Holy Spirit gives us the power to tell others that Jesus loves them, that He is their Savior; and He wants them to be in heaven too.

Know Who the Gift Is From

The Word
Jesus said, "All that My Father has is Mine; that is why I said that the Spirit will take what I give Him and tell it to you." John 16:15 (From the Gospel for the First Sunday After Pentecost)

The World
A plate of homemade cookies.

We know there is one God. But God speaks about Himself as three persons. How three can be one and one can be three is impossible for us to understand. And this sermon won't explain it to you. But God wants us to know Him as the Father and the Son and the Holy Spirit.

Our Bible reading for today refers to all three persons of God. In it Jesus tells us one of the reasons we should know God as Father, Son, and Holy Spirit. He wants us to know where our gifts from God come from. We need to know who to thank for those gifts. Jesus says, "All that My Father has is Mine; that is why I said that the Spirit will take what I give Him and tell it to you."

Everything God the Father has belongs to Jesus also. When Jesus sends the Holy Spirit to give His gifts to us, the gifts of a new life, of love, hope, and many others, those gifts come from Jesus even though the Holy Spirit delivers them. If they come from Jesus, they also come from God the Father.

To help understand, let's suppose you wanted to give your teacher some cookies. Your mother would make the cookies. She might use money that your father earned to buy the sugar, eggs, and whatever else is included in the cookies. Then you'd give the cookies to the teacher.

Now, I ask you, who are the cookies from? You gave them to the teacher; so they are a gift from you. But your mother made them; so they are a gift from her. But your father earned the money to buy the ingredients; so the cookies are from him. When you think about it, the cookies are a gift from all of you, from your family.

God is not a family. There is only one God. God is our Father who creates all things; so everything we have comes from Him. God is the Son Jesus who paid for our sins so we could live with God now and forever. Without Jesus we would be separated from God; so everything we have comes from Him. The Holy Spirit tells us about Jesus and gives us faith. Without Him, we would not know what Jesus has done for us.

So our gifts are from God, the love, forgiveness, peace, eternal life, and more, are gifts from God the Father, God the Son, and God the Holy Spirit. We do not need to understand God to receive His gifts. But we need to know Him; so we can know that the gifts are real. We have them because God gave them to us. Then we know who to thank.

Jesus Tells You What to Do Because . . .

The Word
[A Roman officer sent a message to Jesus and said,] "I, too, am a man placed under the authority of superior officers, and I have soldiers under me. I order this one, 'Go!' and he goes; I order that one, 'Come!' and he comes; and I order my slave, 'Do this!' and he does it." Luke 7:8 (From the Gospel for the Second Sunday After Pentecost)

The World
Two potted houseplants.

An officer in the Roman army wanted Jesus to heal his servant. But the Roman did not go to Jesus; he sent a message. The officer explained that he knew what it was like to have someone tell him what to do, and he knew how to tell others what to do. He knew Jesus had the same authority. So he asked Jesus to heal his servant. Jesus was amazed at the Roman's faith. Jesus did what the man asked. He healed the servant.

We also understand that Jesus has the authority to make things happen. We know He is God. He has the power to make us well. He has the authority to tell us what we are to do and what we are not to do.

But remember the Roman officer knew not only that Jesus had the power to tell others what to do, but he also knew that Jesus had others who told Him what to do. Jesus not only had authority, but also responsibility.

We know Jesus has authority over us. Do you also know that Jesus lives under authority? Let's use an illustration to understand this.

Suppose this houseplant belongs to your mother. You ask if you can pick a flower (or leaf) from it. Your mother says no, you cannot, because it is her plant. Only she has the authority to use her plant.

But your mother gives you this plant. It is yours. Now you have the authority to do what you want with it. You can put it where you want it. You can pick flowers from it. But because you have the right to do what you want with it, you are also responsible for it. If you don't water it, it will die. If you put it in the wrong place, it will not grow. Because it is yours you have the authority to do what you want with it, but you are also responsible for it.

Jesus has authority over you because He is responsible for you. When Jesus gave His life for you, He accepted responsibility for you. He can tell you what to do, because He has taken care of you. He has taken the responsibility for anything you do wrong. He has accepted the responsibility to bring you back to life after you die.

We are glad that Jesus is responsible for us. But sometimes we don't want Him to have authority over us. But remember—authority and responsibility always go together. You can do what you want with the plant because you must take care of it. If you don't want Jesus to tell you what to do, you are also saying you don't want Him to be responsible for you.

Jesus does not give up His responsibility for you. He doesn't give up on you if you fail to accept His authority. He has taken the responsibility of staying with you. When you accept His authority, you are receiving all the good things He wants to give to you.

The Funeral That Didn't Last

The Word
Jesus said, "Young man! Get up, I tell you!" The dead man sat up and began to talk, and Jesus gave him back to his mother. Luke 7:14, 15 (From the Gospel for the Third Sunday After Pentecost)

The World
The empty container of a frozen food item, an ice chest, ice.

I had to bring this ice chest because I want to show you this (the empty container). Since I took it out of the refrigerator at home, I had to keep it cold. You know what happens if frozen food is allowed to thaw. If it is not used, it will spoil. So I have to keep this in an ice chest with ice.

After you've seen how much work I went to to keep the food from thawing, I want you to see something. (Open the container.) See—it is empty. I didn't need the ice chest and ice, because there is nothing to keep cold.

Just as I went to a lot of trouble that was unnecessary, some people in our Bible story went to a lot of trouble to take care of something that needed no care. A woman in the town of Nain was sad because her only son had died. Her husband was already dead. All of her family and friends were sad for her. They came to help her bury her son. They planned a nice funeral. They got a coffin and a tomb. They covered the body with spices. Then they carried him to the grave.

But as they walked along the road, they met Jesus. He said, "Young man! I tell you, get up!" And the dead man got up. He was alive!

Jesus ruined the funeral at Nain that day. You can't have a funeral unless someone is dead. The coffin, the spices, the grave were all unnecessary because they had no one to bury; just as the ice chest and ice were unnecessary because the frozen food box was empty.

We also have funerals today. Our funerals are not exactly like the one in Nain. We have flowers at funerals today. Our coffins are different, but they serve the same purpose. Our graves are different, but they also serve the same purpose. But one thing is exactly the same—we can't have a funeral unless someone is dead.

Just as Jesus changed the funeral at Nain, He also changes the funerals today. He promises us that we also will be raised from the dead. Because He died in our place, our death is not permanent. Our death is only temporary. Because Jesus rose from the dead; so also we will be raised from the dead.

When we plan funerals, we don't have to build a monument that will last forever. We don't have to take care of the body as though we are making it comfortable. All of our efforts are as wasted as keeping an empty box frozen. The grave is only temporary. We show love and respect for the body of the person who died. But we remember that Jesus is the one who is taking care of that loved one. And Jesus does just give us a good funeral. He ruins funerals by giving us a life that never ends.

To Give, You Must First Receive

The Word

"There were two men who owed money to a moneylender," Jesus began. "One owed him five hundred silver coins, and the other one fifty. Neither of them could pay him back, so he canceled the debts of both. Which one, then, will love him more?" Luke 7:41, 42 (From the Gospel for the Fourth Sunday After Pentecost)

The World

Two empty cardboard milk cartons, a small glass of water, a large glass of water.

God loves all people. He offers all of us the same love. But some people love God more than others do. We have a hard time understanding our own love for God. We can't measure it like we measure how tall we are or how much we weigh. We have even a more difficult time trying to understand how others love God. We want to help them have more love for God. But we don't want to judge them by saying they don't love Him enough.

In our Bible reading for today, Jesus explains why a woman who had committed many sins could love Him so much and why others, who thought they were good, did not give Him much love. He told a story about a man who owed a moneylender 500 silver coins and another who owed 50. The moneylender canceled both debts. Then Jesus asked which of the two who owed money would love the moneylender the most. The answer, of course, is the one who had owed the larger debt. He received more; so He loved more.

We can see Jesus' parable this way. See these two empty milk cartons. I'll pour a small glass of water into this one—and a large glass of water into this one. Now if you were thirsty for a big drink of water, which carton would you drink from? This one, of course. You'll get more water out of the one that had the most water put in. Neither carton can give more than it received.

We are like the milk cartons, and the water is like love. The more love we receive, the more we can give. If we have only a little love poured in us, then we can only pour a little out. Remember the Bible tells us that we love God because He first loved us. He poured love into us when He gave us His Son, Jesus Christ. Because He loves us, we can love Him and other people.

So when we want to measure our love for God, or when we want to help someone else love God more, we cannot start by telling ourselves or others that we ought to love God more. No one can give what he has not received. Instead we start by telling ourselves and others how much love God has given us. When we receive the love, we can then give it.

Don't misunderstand the story Jesus told by thinking that if you sin more you will have more forgiveness and then love God more. God not only helps you when He forgives your sins through Jesus, but He also sends His Holy Spirit to help you avoid sin. He gives you love when you do sin; because in His love He forgives you. He gives you love when you do not sin; because His power helps you avoid the evils of sin.

God also loves you in many other ways. He guides you in life. He gives you joy and happiness. He stays with you in sorrow and problems. Look at all the ways God wants to love you, then you will be filled with His love. And you will be able to love Him even more.

Forget Yourself to Find the Way

The Word

And He [Jesus] said to them all, "If anyone wants to come with Me, he must forget himself, take up his cross every day, and follow Me." Luke 9:23
(From the Gospel for the Fifth Sunday After Pentecost)

The World

Two tickets and two crosses.

I'm going on a pretend trip to Disneyland. Since this is a pretend trip, I want each of you to imagine that you are going with me. But I'll ask Kurt to come with me. Here's your ticket, Kurt. And here is mine. Since you are going with me, you might leave your ticket here. (Take the ticket from him and lay it down.)

As we go on the trip (walk with the child), we come to many places where we have to decide which way to go. (Stop at an aisle where you could turn several ways.) Which way would you like to go, Kurt, this way or that? No, that's the wrong way, pretend Disneyland is that way.

Now we are at Disneyland. Here is my ticket. I can go in. But you left yours back there. It is too late to go back to get it. You don't get to go in.

That was only a pretend trip. But in our Bible reading for today Jesus invites you to go on a real trip with Him. He says, "If anyone wants to come to Me, . . ." Do you want to go with Jesus? To be with Him now and forever in heaven? If so, listen to what He tells you.

First, He says you must forget yourself. If you are going with Jesus, you can't think about the way you want to go. You have to forget yourself. You go the way He leads. When we are traveling with Jesus, we will come to many places in the road like the places where Kurt and I had to stop and decide which way to go. You will have to decide: Do I have time to read the Bible and worship God; or do I have other things I'd rather do? Am I willing to love the people Jesus loves, or do I hate and ignore them? Do I want to live my life my own way, or do I want to live my life His way? Jesus says we are to forget ourselves and follow Him.

But that's not all. He also says we must take up our cross every day and follow Him. Jesus had a cross for Himself. (Show the first cross.) He was able to return to heaven because He died for us on the cross to take away our guilt. He took the responsibility for our sins when He suffered and died on the cross.

Because He has saved us, He also gives us crosses. Each of you imagine that you have this cross. You will not have to die on your cross. Jesus has already done that for all of us. But we who have the blessings of His cross also share in the responsibility of giving those blessings to others. We have to carry our crosses to show that we have forgiveness from Jesus, and we also give forgiveness to others. When we lay our crosses down, we refuse to help others. By doing that, we are also refusing the cross that helps us.

Jesus invites you to forget yourself, pick up your cross every day and follow Him. When you accept that invitation, you are not only going to heaven to be with Jesus—you are with Him now.

Keep Your Eyes on Jesus

The Word

Jesus said to him, "Anyone who starts to plow and then keeps looking back is of no use for the Kingdom of God." Luke 9:62 (From the Gospel for the Sixth Sunday After Pentecost)

The World

If the children are in a group, ask all to participate, or ask one to represent all.

Jesus invites us to follow Him. He leads us to heaven. He also leads us to do many things with Him while we are here on earth. We cannot follow Jesus unless we watch where He is going.

In our Bible reading Jesus is talking to a man who said he wanted to follow Jesus, but he had some other things he had to do first. Jesus says, "Anyone who starts to plow and then keeps looking back is of no use for the Kingdom of God."

In those days the farmers guided the plow while the oxen pulled it. If the farmer did not watch where he was going, the plow would come up out of the soil, or would hit a rock or stump. The farmer couldn't look around at the scenery. He had to watch where he was going. Jesus said that those who follow Him also have to keep their eyes on what they are doing. They can't look back at other things.

Maybe you've never plowed with oxen, but you can understand what Jesus is telling you. I'll ask you to look at me. You do what I do. (Raise one hand.) That is easy. (Touch your nose.) As long as you watch me, you can do what I do. But now I want all of you to look the other way. (While they are looking away, touch your ear and fold your hands.) Now you can't do what I do. If you look in the other direction, you can't follow me.

We also have to look at Jesus if we are to follow Him. We look at Jesus when we study about Him to see how He lived and how He treated people. When we look at Him, we see that He was kind to people; so we can be kind to others also. When we look at Him, we see that He helped people; so we can help others. When we look to Jesus, we receive the love He has for us; so we can give the love to others. Jesus not only shows us how to live; He also gives us the power to live that way.

But sometimes we forget to look at Jesus. Other things distract us. Other things take our attention away from Him. We follow what other people do instead of what Jesus does. That becomes a problem. Jesus tells us that if we keep looking back we are of no use for the kingdom of God.

Notice that Jesus said, "then keeps looking back." All of us look away from Him some. But when we do, we can remember that He is the one who forgives us. So we look back to Jesus to receive forgiveness. Then we are looking at Him again, and we follow Him.

How Does God Talk to You?

The Word
Jesus said to His disciples: "Whoever listens to you listens to Me; whoever rejects you rejects Me; and whoever rejects Me rejects the one who sent Me." Luke 10:16 (From the Gospel for the Seventh Sunday After Pentecost)

The World
A covered cross on the altar, and a paper cross for each child.

Most people believe there is a God. But many say they do not feel close to God. They don't hear God talk to them. He is far away from them. But God wants to talk to us. He wants to be near us. And God tells us that He has a way of speaking to us. Listen to what Jesus says in our Bible reading, "Whoever listens to you listens to Me; whoever rejects you rejects Me; and whoever rejects Me rejects the one who sent Me."

Let's start with this (the covered cross). It is the message God has for us. Because we have sinned, we are far from God and cannot hear His message. That's why it is covered. (Ask a child to uncover the cross and bring it close to the other children.) But Jesus came to earth to bring the message of God to all people. Jesus showed the world God's love. We use the cross as a sign of God's message because it reminds us that Jesus died to pay for our sins and rose again to tell us that we will live forever with God.

When people saw Jesus, they received God's message in their lives. (Ask the child holding the cross to give each of the others a paper cross.) Now they have the message of God's love not only for themselves but also to give to others. Notice what has happened. Jesus brought the message to us; so we can see how God loves us. Now we have that love to give to others.

That's why Jesus told His disciples that anyone who listened to what they had to say about Jesus was really listening to Jesus. And anyone who rejected the disciples' message from Jesus was rejecting Jesus and also God. God sent Jesus to deliver His love to us. Jesus gave us God's love and sent others to tell the rest of the world how God offers love and forgiveness to everyone.

This Bible lesson has two messages for us. First, we need to know how God talks to us. He speaks to us through the message of Jesus Christ. And we receive that message from those who believe in Jesus and who share that message with us. Anytime we listen to others who tell us about Christ, we are listening to the Savior. If we reject those who tell us about Jesus, we are rejecting the Savior.

The second lesson is that we are also to tell others the story of God's love for us in Christ. You also have the cross. You have something to tell others. Those who hear your message of Christ will be hearing Christ. Those who reject your love in Christ will be rejecting Christ.

Take the cross with you as a reminder that you have heard God speak to you through others and that you can speak the message from God to others.

Ask the Right Question

The Word

But the teacher of the Law wanted to justify himself, so he asked Jesus, "Who is my neighbor?" Luke 10:29 (From the Gospel for the Eighth Sunday After Pentecost)

The World

A box of books including two paperbacks, a moderately priced book, an expensive art book, and an antique book.

Here is a box of books. Suppose I tell you I'll give you a dollar if you take the box to my house. But let's also suppose that on the way to my house you meet some of your friends. So you put the box down and play with the friends. When you come back, the box is gone. You lost my books.

What would you do? When you make a mistake, you have to pay for it. So you might ask me how much the books cost, so you could pay for them. I'd tell you the price of the books. First there were two paperbacks (show them). They were used; so they'd be worth about 50¢ each. That's one dollar. Can you pay that? Then there was a book my son gave me for Father's Day. It costs $9. Maybe you have that much in a coin bank. Then there was an art book. It was printed in color—that costs a lot. This book is worth $29. Maybe you have a savings account or have something you could sell for $29. The last book is an antique. It is worth $500. Do you have that much money?

You asked if you could pay for the books, and I said you could. But now you realize you asked the wrong question. You can't pay for the books—not because I won't let you, but because you don't have the money. You would have to ask if your parents or their insurance company could pay for the books.

In our Bible story for today a man also asked the wrong question. He asked Jesus what he had to do to receive eternal life. Jesus asked the man what the Bible said. The man said He must love God and his neighbor. Jesus said, "You are right, do this and you will live."

Jesus' answer was like my saying you can pay for the books. You had better find out how much the books cost. The man wanted to know who he had to love; so he asked, "Who is my neighbor?" Jesus told him the story of the Good Samaritan. In the story Jesus shows that anyone who needs help is your neighbor. If the man was to save himself, he had to love and help every person in need.

The man could have loved a few people, like you could have paid for some of the books. But he could not love and help all people. He would need someone to help him do that; just as you needed someone to help you pay for the books.

Jesus helped the man see he had asked the wrong question. He had asked, "What must I do to receive eternal life?" He wanted to earn it for himself. After the man saw the price, he had to ask God, "What will You do to give me eternal life?"

And God answers that question. He sent Jesus to love all people and to save all people. Jesus did love us as He loved Himself. He gave His life for us. Because He has loved us, we can depend on Him for our salvation. And we can love our neighbor because He helps us.

You Have a Choice

The Word
The Lord answered her, "Martha, Martha! You are worried and troubled over so many things, but just one is needed. Mary has chosen the right thing, and it will not be taken away from her." Luke 10:41, 42 (From the Gospel for the Ninth Sunday After Pentecost)

The World
A math textbook, paper, pencils, eraser, ruler.

A teacher gave the class a special homework assignment. Everyone had to do the problems on page 47 of the textbook (show it). The students all knew it was an important assignment. Tom wanted to make sure he did it just right. He got out paper, several pencils (just in case the point broke on one), an eraser. He even took a ruler because he knew the teacher wanted the problems to be written in straight columns. He took all of this home with him. But he forgot the math textbook. So even though he had all this stuff, he couldn't do the homework. Other students who took nothing but the textbook were able to do the work.

Tom wanted to do the homework, but he took home the wrong things. He made the wrong choice. The other students who took home their textbooks made the right choice. They chose the important thing while Tom chose what was not necessary.

You and I have to make many choices in our lives. Often we choose the things that are not necessary and forget the things that are important. Jesus helps us make the right choices in our lives. In the Bible reading for today He had gone to visit two sisters, Mary and Martha. Both sisters were glad to see Jesus. Each had a choice to make. Mary chose to listen to Jesus. She sat down with Him, and He told her what He was doing. He explained how His work was fulfilling all the Old Testament promises that a Messiah would come.

But Martha chose to fix a dinner for Jesus. She rushed out to the kitchen and started to work. She was angry that her sister did not help her; so she complained to Jesus. Jesus answered, "Martha, Martha! You are worried and troubled over so many things, but just one is needed. Mary has chosen the right thing, and it will not be taken away from her."

It was okay for Martha to fix dinner. Jesus ate the dinner. But the dinner was not more important than the message of love and forgiveness that Jesus came to share with the sisters.

You also have to figure out what is most important in your life. Life offers many wonderful and exciting things to do. You can enjoy those things. But remember that the message of Jesus' love for you is also wonderful and exciting. Being with friends is important and good. And being with Jesus is very important and also fun.

Mary listened to Jesus because she wanted to, not because she had to. She had a choice. You also have the choice. God won't force you to read His Word and hear His message. But when you know what He wants to say to you, you'll want to listen to Him.

God's Catalog

The Word

Jesus said to them, "When you pray, say this: 'Father: May Your holy name be honored; may Your Kingdom come. Give us day by day the food we need. Forgive us our sins, for we forgive everyone who does us wrong. And do not bring us to hard testing.'" Luke 11:2-4 (From the Gospel for the Tenth Sunday After Pentecost)

The World

Several small catalogs with order blanks and a "Lord's Prayer" catalog (a pattern of the prayer written on each page) with an "order blank" (list of the petitions) at the back.

When the disciples asked Jesus to teach them how to pray, He gave them the prayer we call "The Lord's Prayer." In His prayer He tells us what He wants to give us. He asks us to use the prayer so we can pray for the things we need the most and the things He wants to give us.

We can look at the prayer as though it were an order blank in a catalog. You've seen catalogs like these. This one shows special gifts. In the back is an order blank listing the things available through the catalog. This catalog shows camping equipment and in the back is an order blank. This one lists office supplies—it also has an order blank. I am showing you these catalogs to remind you that you would have to use the right order blank with the right catalog. You wouldn't order gifts with the order blank from the business supply catalog. You wouldn't order camping equipment from the catalog of gifts.

When Jesus gives us this sample of a prayer, He is giving us the order blank that goes with His catalog. All of the gospels are the catalog. The gospels show us what God wants to give us in Jesus Christ. First (show page with verse 2a), God wants us to know Him through Jesus. Jesus became a person who lived on earth; so we could know God and honor Him. Next (verse 2b) God offers us His power in our present life. He says His kingdom can be with us now, because Christ has made the kingdom of God for our hearts. He wants to give us food and the other things we need in our daily lives (verse 3). He wants to forgive our sins (verse 4a). Jesus has paid for all of our sins, so we can receive forgiveness for ourselves and we can forgive others. He also wants to protect us from falling into temptations and other difficult problems (verse 4b).

God offers us many other gifts. But those listed in this order blank are His "specials." He knows we have a special need for them. And He sent Christ to be our Savior as a special way of filling these needs for us.

As you pray the Lord's Prayer think of it as an order blank from God. It shows you what He wants to give you and what He thinks you need. Look at each item and realize how much you need God's help. Only God can give you the things on this order blank. You can't find them in other catalogs.

You may also ask Him for other things. But start first with this list. After you have received the things that are most important, you will have a better understanding of the other things you want. You will also know that God loves you and wants to give you what is best for you.

Don't Be Fooled by Money

The Word

And He [Jesus] went on to say to them all, "Watch out and guard yourselves from every kind of greed; because a person's true life is not made up of the things he owns, no matter how rich he may be." Luke 12:15 (From the Gospel for the Eleventh Sunday After Pentecost)

The World

A new, expensive toy that children would enjoy; an inexpensive, worn-out plastic toy; 10 dollars in bills, rubber bands.

If I were to offer you one of these toys, which would you take? All of you would probably choose the new one. It would last for a long time. The other one wasn't as nice even when it was new. Now it is old and worn out. It is ready to be thrown away.

But I know a way to make you choose the old toy. Watch. (Fasten the money to the old toy with the rubber bands.) Now which toy would you rather have? The money makes the old toy look a lot better, doesn't it? With that much money, you could buy a toy like the new one and still have some left over. If you were asked to choose now, you'd probably take the old one.

So I'll give it to you. (Take off the money and offer the toy.) Remember, I asked you which toy you wanted. The money is not a part of the toy. All you get is the worn-out toy.

The worthless toy looked valuable when it had money wrapped around it. But it is worthless without the money. Jesus warns us in our Bible reading not to look at people by how much money they have wrapped around them. He says, "a person's true life is not made up of the things he owns, no matter how rich he may be." Sometimes we wrap money and the things money buys around ourselves to make us look more important. If you feel you are worthless by yourself, like the old toy, you probably need money, fancy clothes, and other things that cost a lot to make you feel important. You become greedy if you think you need those things to make others like you, or even for you to like yourself. Jesus tells us, "Watch out and guard yourselves from every kind of greed."

Greed hurts you because it makes you think your value is in what you own rather than what you are. This cheap old toy is a cheap old toy no matter how much money is wrapped around it. The person who is a sinner is a sinner no matter how much money he has.

Instead of trying to cover our faults with money and the things money buys, we can admit that, by ourselves, we are like the old toy. But God loves us. He sent His Son to make us new people. When Jesus came to be our Savior, He did not cover up our guilt and sin. He forgave us. He removed our faults. He made us new people.

You and I are important—not because of what we own—but because God has made us and still claims us to be His. God thinks you are so important that He sent His Son to die for you. He thinks you are so important that He has prepared a place in heaven for you so you can be with Him forever. Your real value is not in what you own, but in who you are in Jesus Christ.

Know Where Your Heart Is

The Word
Jesus said, "For your heart will always be where your riches are." Luke 12:34 (From the Gospel for the Twelfth Sunday After Pentecost)

The World
A piece of thin cardboard with a tic-tac-toe grid on either side. Number the sections of one grid 1 through 9. Label the other sections: TV, sports, music, friends, Jesus, money, fame, clothes, ?. Also a magnet and a metal washer.

Please play a game with me. (Show the numbered side of the gameboard.) I want you to tell me what position the marker (magnet) is on. If I place it here, it is 3. Here it is 6. Except, I'm going to put the marker on the back side of the game board. Now you can't see where it is.

But you can still know where it is. Did you notice the marker was a magnet? If I put this metal washer on your side of the gameboard, the magnet will hold it in place. When I move the magnet on the back side, the washer on the front side moves. Even though you can't see the magnet back here, you know it is at 4, now it is at 7.

Let's use this game to understand something about ourselves. In our Bible reading Jesus says, "For your heart will always be where your riches are." Jesus isn't talking about where your heart is in your body. Jesus meant that your heart shows what you love, what is most important to you. When you see where your heart is, you know what is most important to you.

But you can't always see where your heart is. (Turn the gameboard over.) Here are some of the places your heart might be. (Talk about the different things that people love. The section with the question mark is for each person to put in his own special interests.)

But you can't see where your heart is. It's on the back side. But you can see where you spend your time and money. You can know what you think and dream about. You can know what gets the most attention in your life. The washer shows how you spend your time and money. It shows what you are interested in. It also shows where your heart is. The heart guides you when you select the things that are most important. If it moves to here, money is most important. You can see where your heart is by how you live for money. Or if clothes are most important to you, your heart moves to here—and the washer shows your attention is on clothes. Or on sports, or TV, or any of the other things.

Jesus wants your heart to be with Him. But if you move your heart to Jesus, your attention, the way you spend your time and money will also move to Him. Notice that all the other things on the gameboard are not bad. They are a good part of your life. But your life should not be centered on any of them. It should be centered on Jesus. Look at your life. How often do you direct your attention to Jesus? Do you come back to Him, not only every week, but every day and every hour?

If you have trouble keeping Jesus in the center of your life, remember that He made you the center of His life. He showed what was most important to Him when He died for all people, including you and me. His heart is with you. And yours can be with Him.

Move to Where the Peace Is

The Word

Jesus asked, "Do you suppose that I came to bring peace to the world? No, not peace, but division." Luke 12:51 (From the Gospel for the Thirteenth Sunday After Pentecost)

The World

An umbrella.

We often call Jesus the Prince of Peace. When He was born, the angels sang about peace on earth. Before He died, He told His disciples He was leaving peace with them. But listen to what Jesus says in our Bible reading for today, "Do you suppose that I came to bring peace to the world? No, not peace, but division."

How can the Prince of Peace say that He did not come to bring peace? We need to think about what Jesus said. Notice, first of all, He did not say we will not have peace. He wants us to have peace. That's why He died for us. He has forgiven our sins so we can be at peace with Him and also be at peace with ourselves and with other people. We can forgive others and we can know others forgive us. That is peace.

But Jesus says that the peace He gives to us will not bring peace to the world. Many people will not want His peace. They don't want to be forgiven, and they don't want to forgive. That causes division instead of peace.

Can it be true that Jesus wants us to have peace but that He did not come to bring peace to the world? Yes, it can. Let's look at it this way. Let's pretend that all of you are in the car that is out in the church parking lot. Let's also suppose it is raining very hard. I want you to come into the church so you can worship. But you don't want to get wet. And I don't want you to get wet. I would take this umbrella and run out to the car. Then you could come to the church with me under the umbrella. That way you would not get wet.

I would not take the umbrella out to the car so you could stay out in the parking lot. Instead I would go out there to bring you back in here. If someone refused to get out of the car because he didn't want to walk under the umbrella, that person would stay out in the rain. It would cause a division.

Because we are sinners in a sinful world, we are like a car full of people out in the parking lot in a rainstorm. We can't come into heaven (is it OK if we call the church heaven?) by ourselves. So Jesus comes out to get us. He offers us the umbrella of His love and peace. But He did not take His love and peace out there so we could stay out there. Rather He took it out there to bring us back here. He did not come to bring peace to the world but to bring peace to all who would believe in Him, so they could live at peace with Him forever in heaven.

We can have peace now even while we are waiting to go to heaven. But we have that peace only because Christ has come out to be with us. He shares His peace with us. Enjoy that peace now. And remember that we are moving to the place of peace forever.

Know Who Will Open the Door

The Word
Jesus answered them, "Do your best to go in through the narrow door; because many people will surely try to go in but will not be able." Luke 13:24 (From the Gospel for the Fourteenth Sunday After Pentecost)

The World
A set of keys and a door which is a part of the worship area. (If no door is available, make one from heavy cardboard. The door must be larger than the opening; so it can open only one way.)

I would like all of the kids to come over by this door. In our Bible reading for today Jesus talks about a door. His door is the one that leads to heaven. You know that this door only goes to _____. But let's pretend that heaven is on the other side of this door. All of us would be eager to go through that door.

So let's do it. (Try to open the door, but pull if it is a door that opens outward or push if it is a door that opens inward.) I can't get the door open. Maybe I need a key. But these keys don't fit that lock. Maybe if we pulled together we could open it. (Discuss the problem with the kids. Let them discover that the door must be opened the other way.)

See—it is easy to open the door when I do it the right way. That's why I wanted you to think about the door to heaven. Jesus tells us in our Bible reading that many people will not be able to go through the door to heaven. I want each of you to be able to open that door. And much more important—God wants you to come through the door to heaven.

If God wants us in heaven, we have to ask why some won't be able to go through the door. They won't be able to go through for the same reason we couldn't open this door at first.

We were trying to do it the wrong way. Many people try to get into heaven the wrong way. They want to save themselves. They want to go to heaven because they think they have earned it. They want their own key or their own strength to open the door. Jesus tells those people they will never be able to open the door.

But God has opened the door for us. Jesus came from heaven (open the door) to be on earth with us. (Close the door.) He lived here and earned the way for us to go back through the door. He has the key that opens it. He has the strength to make it possible for us to be in heaven. When He died and rose again, He opened the door (do it) through death to the life that lasts forever. (Close the door.)

Even though the door is closed now, you need not be afraid. Jesus will open it for you. He invites you to be with Him forever.

Give to Those Who Can't Give

The Word

Then Jesus said to His host, "When you give a lunch or a dinner, do not invite your friends or your brothers or your relatives or your rich neighbors—for they will invite you back, and in this way you will be paid for what you did. When you give a feast, invite the poor, the crippled, the lame, and the blind; and you will be blessed, because they are not able to pay you back. God will repay you on the day the good people rise from death." Luke 14:12-14 (From the Gospel for the Fifteenth Sunday After Pentecost)

The World

A handful of coins to match what the children might have. Arrange ahead of time for some of the children to have money with them.

How much money do you have? If you have any change, take it out of your pocket or purse and hold it in your hand. This is the money I have (show coins). I'm going to give this money to some of you. I'm willing to give my money away.

Which one of you has a dime? Mike has a dime. So I'll give him a dime. Now, Mike, since I gave you a dime, will you give me yours? (Do the same with several children, always giving them the amount you can receive back from them.)

I feel good because I've been giving my money away. Jesus tells us to share—and I've been sharing. But have I really given anything away? I still have the same amount of money that I started with. I've only traded money with some of you. In our Bible reading Jesus tells us that we are not helping people when we only trade with them. If I feed only those who also feed me, I'm helping myself not others. If I will help only those who will help me, then I'm really just taking care of myself.

Jesus wants us to help people who need help. They are the

ones who can't pay us back for the help we give. Everyone likes to give gifts to those who give them gifts. But because we know and follow Jesus, we can do more than that. We can also give gifts to those who can't return them.

We can help others because Jesus has helped us. When He came to be a part of our lives, He gave Himself for all people. He didn't say He would help only those who were good, or those who were sincere, or those who tried hard. He wants to help everyone. He died for the world. He offers eternal life to all who will believe in Him.

When you know that Jesus loves you that much and that He is taking care of you, you can help others. You can love others and share the love you have from Jesus with them. You love them, not because they have deserved it, or that they will pay you back, but because you have received the love from Jesus, so you can in like manner give it to them. Jesus will always give you more.

Plan to Finish the Job

The Word

Jesus said: "Whoever does not carry his own cross and come after Me cannot be My disciple. If one of you is planning to build a tower, he sits down first and figures out what it will cost, to see if he has enough money to finish the job. If he doesn't, he will not be able to finish the tower after laying the foundation; and all who see what happened will make fun of him." Luke 14:27-29 (From the Gospel for the Sixteenth Sunday After Pentecost)

The World

A small banner (about 18 inches high), a stack of styrofoam coffee cups (about 20 inches high), a pin.

A Sunday school teacher brought this banner to class. (Talk about its message.) However, the teacher forgot to bring a stand to hold the banner. She wanted it on the table, but it won't stand by itself.

A student said he could make a stand. He had a clever idea. He knew there were cups like this (show one) in the kitchen. Just before the class started, he brought a stack of cups to the classroom. (Show enough cups, separated from one another, to make a 12-inch stack.) He put the cups together, stuck a pin in the top to hold the banner. But look—he did not have enough cups. The student had a good idea, but he didn't have enough cups to finish the job.

In our Bible reading Jesus tells us we should plan our lives so we can finish the job. He said, "If one of you is planning to build a tower, he sits down first and figures out what it will cost, to see if he had enough money to finish the job. If he doesn't, he will not be able to finish the tower after laying the foundation; and all who see what happened will make fun of him."

Jesus is telling us that if we start our lives as Christians, we should plan to continue to live as Christians. He said, "Whoever does not carry his own cross and come after Me, cannot be My disciple."

At your baptism you were given a cross—not just a metal or wooden cross, but a message that you can feel. It is the message that Christ died for you and rose again. That cross is the foundation of your spiritual life—the first cup in the tower (take one cup).

But Jesus tells us that to be His disciples we must not just receive the cross. We take up the cross and follow Him. We build on to the foundation of faith in Jesus. (Add another cup to the first.) You build on when you learn more about Jesus in Sunday school or devotions. (Add more cups as you talk until the tower is high enough to hold the banner.) You add on more to your faith as you worship, as you tell others about Jesus, as you love others and help people who are in need.

Jesus tells you to plan your life, so it is complete. See now the tower holds the banner. It is complete. Your life will not be complete until you are in heaven. But today you should be adding to your faith. You know that your faith is a gift from God. As He has given you faith up to now, so also will He give you a faith that will help you finish your life here, so you will live forever with Him.

Praise or Blame for Jesus

The Word

One day when many tax collectors and other outcasts came to listen to Jesus, the Pharisees and the teachers of the Law started grumbling, "This man welcomes outcasts and even eats with them!" Luke 15:1, 2 (From the Gospel for the Seventeenth Sunday After Pentecost)

The World

A sack of assorted children's clothes (some clean, some dirty), two boxes (one labeled "Clean," the other "Dirty"), a box of laundry soap.

Listen to what people said about Jesus in our Bible reading for today: "This man welcomes outcasts and even eats with them!" Do you think the people who said that were praising Jesus? Were they glad that He would be with people who had done wrong? Or were they blaming Him? Were they saying that He should not spend His time with bad people?

Reading the rest of the story, we learn that the people were complaining about Jesus. They thought Jesus was bad because He was with bad people. But Jesus thought He should be with the people who were sinners. He thought their gripe against Him was a compliment to Him.

To understand why Jesus wanted to be with sinners, let's look at this sack of clothes. Some are dirty—they should be put in this box for dirty clothes. Some are clean—they should be put in this box for clean clothes. (Sort out the clothes into the two boxes.)

I also have a box of laundry soap. Which of the two boxes does it go in? The clean clothes don't need soap. But the dirty clothes do. So I'll put the soap with the dirty clothes. Does that mean the soap is dirty? Of course not. It means the soap will make the dirty clothes clean.

Suppose we had two boxes for people. One box for good people. The other for bad. Which box would you go in? We have all done something wrong. Like dirty clothes we all need to be cleaned. But some people try to hide their sins. They want to be in the clean box.

But Jesus comes to the people in the dirty box. He is not a sinner. He is like the soap. He comes to be with those who are sinners, to make them clean.

We can learn two lessons from the soap and the boxes for clothing. First, we learn that we are sinners and we need to be forgiven by Jesus. We can try to pretend we are not sinners. We can make ourselves look clean on the outside. But we all have done something wrong. Christ comes to us to make us holy. He takes away our sin because He died for us. We are clean and holy before God because Jesus is a part of our lives.

We also learn that Jesus wants to help all other people too. When we say He died for sinners, we mean He loves all sinners. We are not to judge other people and say that they are hypocrites—so they shouldn't be in church. We are not to say that some other people's sins are worse than our sins—so the people who do those things can't be with Jesus.

Like the people in our Bible story we can say, "This man welcomes outcasts and even eats with them!" Only instead of complaining because Jesus loves sinners, we say it to thank and praise Him.

But You Can Serve One

The Word
Jesus said, "No servant can be the slave of two masters; he will hate one and love the other; he will be loyal to one and despise the other. You cannot serve both God and money." Luke 16:13 (From the Gospel for the Eighteenth Sunday After Pentecost)

The World
Two toys so large that a child can not carry both at the same time. Suggestions: stuffed animals, beach ball, play furniture.

Let's plan a trip. You are going to visit a friend, and you want to take a toy with you. First, you decide to take this stuffed bear. He's big and difficult to carry, but he's nice to play with, and if you want to take a nap, he makes a nice pillow.

But as you go out the door, you see your beach ball. You and your friend could play with the ball together. That would be fun.

But now you have a problem. You want to take the bear, and you want to take the ball. But they are both big. You can't carry them at the same time. You have to decide to take one or the other. Or you could get disgusted and leave them both at home.

As you take your trip through life, you will also have to decide what you want to take with you. The world offers you many nice things. You can fill your arms with clothes, houses, record players, toys, bicycles, books, food. All of those things become like the teddy bear. They fill your arms.

But as you think about your life, you also remember that you need God. He came to be part of you when He lived on earth and died for your sins. The Savior gives you love, joy, peace, forgiveness, hope, and even eternal life. All of those things are also like a big toy. They fill your life up.

Now you have a problem. You can't carry at the same time the things the world says are important and the things that God says are important. Each is a load in itself.

We can have both God and money. But we cannot serve both. Each is too large to be shared with the other. If you only care about fun and the things of this world, you will forget God who is preparing you to live also in another world. If you remember what God has promised and how much He loves you, you will not want to serve the things that seem important only for now.

Each day you must decide whom you will serve. The world will offer you an armful of joys and an armful of cares. But don't serve them. Just use them for your day-by-day life. God will offer you armsful of love and hope. Accept them and use them because they will last forever.

Jesus says that you can't serve two masters. But you can serve One. You can serve the God who has served you.

What Gets Your Attention?

The Word

[Jesus was telling a story about a man in hell who asked Abraham to send someone to warn his five brothers.] Jesus said, "Abraham said, 'Your brothers have Moses and the prophets to warn them; your brothers should listen to what they say.' The rich man answered, 'That is not enough, father Abraham! But if someone were to rise from death to go to them, then they would turn from their sins.' But Abraham said, 'If they will not listen to Moses and the prophets, they will not be convinced even if someone were to rise from death.'" Luke 16:29-31 (From the Gospel for the Nineteenth Sunday After Pentecost)

The World

A Bible, a small note (message below) and a poster made with bright colors and pictures saying, "Glad You're Home."

Two mothers were shopping one afternoon. Each had a child in school. One mother put this big sign on the door for her child when he came home. The other mother put this little note for her child.

When the kids came home, each found the message. The one who saw this big poster thought, "That's great. Mom really thought about me. I'm glad she didn't leave just a little piece of paper for me."

The other child opened the note. It said, "I have gone shopping and will be back at 4 o'clock. There is a snack for you in the refrigerator. I love you. Mom." The child who got the note knew where his mother was and when she would return. He also had something to eat.

The poster was more flashy and got more attention. But the note was more helpful. Let's apply that idea to the message we get from God. Do you want a flashy message? Or a plain message that gives the information you need?

Our Bible reading comes from a story Jesus told about a man who died and went to hell. The man remembered his brothers back on earth and asked Abraham to send Lazarus back to earth to warn them. But Abraham told the man his brothers could read what Moses and the prophets had written. They would learn that God had promised a Savior who would pay for their sins so all who believed in Him could be saved.

But the man in hell had not read the Bible. He said his brothers would not read it either. But if someone rose from the dead to warn them, they'd believe him. He wanted a big flashy sign for his brothers. But Abraham said the flashy sign won't work. People who won't believe the Bible won't believe those who rise from the dead either.

Jesus told this story so we would listen to Him now. We have His message here in the Bible. We use it each time we are together. It tells us that Jesus came to earth to be our Savior. He has prepared a place for us in heaven.

Some don't like the simple message. They think the Bible is a dull book. They would rather have a miracle to prove God is real. But God does not have to prove He is real. Instead He wants to tell us that He loves us. He wants to give us the information that we need. He wants us to know Him and to believe Him. That's in the note He left for you.

Don't Spread Your Sin Around

The Word
Jesus said to His disciples, "Things that make people fall into sin are bound to happen, but how terrible for the one who makes them happen!" Luke 17:1 (From the Gospel for the Twentieth Sunday After Pentecost)

The World
Mouth spray, handkerchief, and gauze face mask.

Often I bring something for you to look at as we talk about God's Word. Today I want you to look at something so small that you can't see it, but it is there. It is a germ. Pretend that I am sick—though I am feeling fine. But if I had the flu, I would have germs in my mouth and nose. You couldn't see those germs, but if I kissed you, sneezed on you, or maybe even if I touched you, you would get the germs.

I do not want to make you sick; so I would protect you from the germs. I might use this mouth spray. (Do it.) It kills some germs. If I had to sneeze, I would cover my mouth and nose with a handkerchief. (Do it.) That would stop the germs from being spread all over the room. Or if I had a serious illness or was with someone who was in poor health, I would wear a face mask like this (put it on) to keep the germs from spreading.

In our Bible reading Jesus tells us that sin is something like germs. Sin is a part of our lives even when we can't see it. Jesus says, "Things that make people sin are bound to happen." We cannot promise to stop sinning because we are sinful people in a sinful world. Things are going to happen to tempt us to lie, hate, lust, steal, and the like. Things will happen to tempt us not to worship, not to pray, not to tell others about Jesus and His love. Sometimes we will give in to those temptations, and we will sin. Jesus says it's bound to happen.

But Jesus also says, "How terrible for the one who makes them (sins) happen." We can't use the fact that we are sinners as an excuse to make others sin. If I have germs, I do something to stop spreading my germs to others. If I am a sinner, I do something to stop spreading my sin.

We talked about ways to stop spreading germs. Now let's talk about ways to stop spreading sin. Just as this mouth spray kills germs, the Gospel of Jesus Christ kills sin. The Gospel is the power Christ earned for us when He died to pay for our sins and when He rose from the dead to give us a new life. Putting the Gospel on our sins keeps us from spreading our sin to others because it forgives the sin. The sin is dead.

We can stop giving our sins to others by keeping them from being spread to others, as I stopped germs by using the handkerchief and mask. When we brag about our sins, we spread them to others. When we use sin to show off, to make people think we are grown up or cool, we spread them to others. When we try to make others hate whom we hate, or follow our example in bad words or actions, we are spreading sin. Even on the sins that you cannot stop, you can know they are wrong. You can keep from spreading them to others. You can ask Jesus to help you fight against the sin. You can admit to others that the sin is harmful.

Spreading sin is like spreading germs. It hurts people. But sharing the Gospel that forgives sin helps others.

When You Get What You Want

The Word
Jesus spoke up, "There were ten men who were healed; where are the other nine? Why is this foreigner the only one who came back to give thanks to God?" Luke 17:17, 18 (From the Gospel for the Twenty-first Sunday After Pentecost)

The World
Any game for children that two can play.

If you owned a game like this, I'm sure you'd enjoy it. But you can't play this game by yourself. You need a partner. Let's suppose that one of your friends especially likes to play this game. When the friend drops by your house, the two of you always play this game. Each time you see that friend he talks about playing this game.

Since the person has become your best friend, you might decide to give him a present. And what better present could you give than the game? Your friend likes the game. You play together all the time. So you give something that you also like to your friend.

How would you feel if the friend never came to your house again? Instead the friend took the game and played with other kids. When you didn't see much of your friend any more, you would realize that the person really was not your friend. He only wanted to play the game that you had. When he got what he wanted, he didn't want to be with you any more.

Something like this happened in our Bible reading for today. Ten people were very ill. They had a bad skin disease. Not just pimples or an itch—their illness made other people stay away from them. They could only live with others who had the same disease. They came to Jesus and asked Him for help. While they were sick, they needed Jesus and wanted to be with Him.

So Jesus helped them. He cured their sickness. Nine of them were glad to be healed. So glad that they rushed home to their families and friends and forgot all about Jesus. They had what they wanted. They didn't need Jesus any more.

But one of the ten people who was healed remembered who had healed him. He came back to thank Jesus. He also had what He wanted. But when he received what Jesus had to give, he also learned that he wanted more. He wanted to be Jesus' friend. He wanted to stay close to someone who could and would help him.

We also can ask Jesus for help. He wants to help us when we are sick. He wants to help us with school work. He wants to help us get along with our friends. He wants to help us when we have problems. But most of all He wants to be with us, and He wants us to be with Him. He wants to be our friend.

Ask Jesus for help when you need Him. But don't leave Him when you get what you want. Instead stay with Him. He wants to give you more. He wants to continue to love you, and He wants you to love Him.

Knock—Again and Again

The Word
And the Lord continued, "Listen to what that corrupt judge said. Now, will God not judge in favor of His own people who cry to Him day and night for help? Will He be slow to help them? I tell you, He will judge in their favor and do it quickly." Luke 18:6-8a (From the Gospel for the Twenty-second Sunday After Pentecost)

The World
Two doors. Use doors in the worship area or draw them on poster board.

Suppose you visit a friend. You knock on the door of your friend's house. (Do it.) You knock again. (Do it.) How many times would you knock before you decide that your friend was not home? Maybe two or three. Then you would leave.

Now suppose you are coming home from school. You have no key. The door to your house is locked. So you would knock on your own door. (Knock on the other door.) If no one came, you would knock again. And again. Maybe your mother is sleeping. Or maybe she is shopping. But you would knock again. You might play in the yard for a while, but soon you would come back and knock again.

The difference between the two doors is that one is your home and one is the home of a friend. At the friend's house you knock several times and leave. At home you keep on knocking until someone lets you in.

Praying to God is like knocking on a door. When you knock, you are asking someone to let you in. When you pray, you are asking God to come and help you. But when you pray, do you ask a couple of times and then go away—as though you were knocking on someone else's door? Or do you keep on knocking until you get an answer—as though you were knocking on your own door?

Jesus told His followers a story to teach them that they should always pray and never give up. He said a woman kept asking a judge for help. Finally the judged helped her even though he did not like her. Then Jesus explained: "Listen to what the corrupt judge said. Now will God not judge in favor of his people who cry to him day and night for help? Will He be slow to help them? I tell you, He will judge in their favor and do it quickly."

Jesus wants us to knock on His door again and again with our prayers. He does not want us to give up. Sometimes He delays in giving us what we ask for. But He has reasons for waiting. He wants us to think about what we are asking for. Or He wants to give us help in another way. Or He wants us to realize how we must depend upon Him.

Don't give up on your prayers. Ask again and again. Remember God has already given His Son to be your Savior. He gave His life for you. Someone who loves you that much will not turn His back on you. He is the one who told the story of the woman and the judge. He wants you to pray, and He wants to answer your prayer. So knock—again and again.

Which Name Tag Will You Wear?

The Word

Jesus said, "For everyone who makes himself great will be humbled, and everyone who humbles himself will be made great." Luke 18:14b (From the Gospel for the Twenty-third Sunday After Pentecost)

The World

Three large name tags with the following "names" on the front: HERO, GOOD LOOKING and COOL, and on the back: SINNER. Anothr tag with SINNER on the front and SAINT on the back.

I have some name tags that I'd like to give to whoever would like to wear them. This one says "Hero." Here's one that says, "Good Looking," and another that says, "Cool." If you wore tags like these, people would notice you. (Give the tags to children who volunteer to accept them.)

Now I have one name tag left. It says, "Sinner." Does anyone want to wear it? Would you like to wear a sign that says you are a sinner? (If no one will request it, ask a secure child to accept it.)

Even though we don't wear name tags to tell others how great we are, we often try to make ourselves look great. Most of us try to impress other people by what we say and what we do. We want others to think that we are important. When we brag and tell others how great we are, we are doing the same thing as wearing name tags that say, "Hero, Good Looking, or Cool."

In our Bible reading for today Jesus says, "For everyone who makes himself great will be humbled." He says that if we wear a name tag to show how important we are, it will cause us to be ashamed and embarrassed. I want those of you who have name tags that make you look great to turn them over. See what it says on the other side. Sinner. That is also a part of the name tag you chose.

When we try to make ourselves great, Jesus has to come and turn the name tag over. Jesus does not want to hurt us or embarrass us. He wants to help us. He has to help us be honest. He has to show us that we need to depend on Him instead of ourselves. He wants us to know that we need Him to be our Savior. When we build ourselves up, He makes us humble.

Now let's look at the other name tag—the one that said, "Sinner." On the other side it says, "Saint." Jesus also tells us, "Everyone who humbles himself will be made great."

When we admit that we are sinners, Jesus takes away our sin. Then we become saints. Jesus wants us to be humble; so He can make us great. When we know that we must depend on Him, He gives us strength and forgiveness.

Which name tag will you wear? Will you try to make yourself great? Then Jesus will have to teach you to be humble. Will you admit that you are a sinner and need God's help? Then Jesus shares His greatness with you.

Play Show-and-Go-Seek

The Word
[Zacchaeus] was trying to see who Jesus was, but he was a little man and could not see Jesus because of the crowd. So he ran ahead of the crowd and climbed a sycamore tree to see Jesus, who was going to pass that way. Luke 19:3, 4 (From the Gospel for the Twenty-fourth Sunday After Pentecost)

The World
A doll or stick figure of a child.

Have you ever played hide-and-go-seek? In the game one person is "it." Whoever is "it" shuts his eyes while the others hide. If this child (the doll) were playing hide-and-go-seek, he might hide behind me or (suggest other places that the doll could hide).

In our Bible reading for today a man named Zacchaeus played a different kind of game with Jesus. Instead of hide-and-go-seek, he played show-and-go-seek. Instead of hiding from Jesus, he showed himself to Jesus. You and I might try to hide from Jesus some time. So let's talk about the story, so we can also learn to play show-and-go-seek with Jesus.

Zacchaeus was a tax collector and a rich man. From what he said after he met Jesus we know that he was rich because he had cheated others. We also know he was short. Jesus came to the town where Zacchaeus lived. Since Zacchaeus had done bad things, he might have tried to hide from Jesus. Because he was short he could have hidden in the crowd or behind that sycamore tree, and no one would have noticed him. But he knew Jesus was the Savior who forgave sins. He wanted his sins forgiven. He wanted to see Jesus. Instead of hiding from Jesus, he climbed up into a tree. There he saw Jesus. (With the doll show how he could have hidden behind yourself, but instead he crawled up high to see Jesus.)

Because Zacchaeus was up in the tree so he could see Jesus, Jesus could also see him. Jesus spoke to Zacchaeus and asked if He could go to his house for dinner. Zacchaeus said he was sorry for his sins and asked for Jesus' help. Jesus forgave all his sin.

When we do something wrong, we sometimes try to hide from Jesus. If Jesus is the one who is "it" in hide-and-go-seek, He always finds us. He can see anywhere. He is always with us.

The problem is that when we hide from Jesus we cannot see Him. When we hide from Him, we can't hear Him tell us that He loves us and that He forgives us. When we hide from Him, we can't follow Him and be His children.

So instead of playing hide-and-go-seek with Jesus, let's be like Zacchaeus. Let's play show-and-go seek. When we go to seek Jesus, we also show ourselves to Him. When we seek Him, we know He has already found us.

You can show yourself to Jesus when you come to church and Sunday school, when you pray and read your Bible, when you let others know that you believe in the Savior. You show yourself to Jesus when you show others that you believe in Him and love Him.

He Is the God of the Living

The Word
Jesus said, "And Moses clearly proves that the dead are raised to life. In the passage about the burning bush he speaks of the Lord as 'the God of Abraham, the God of Isaac, and the God of Jacob.' He is the God of the living, not of the dead, for to Him all are alive." Luke 20:37, 38 (From the Gospel for the Twenty-fifth Sunday After Pentecost)

The World
A toy stuffed animal, a hypodermic needle (or a fake one).

Let's pretend this stuffed animal is your pet. We'll make it a pet dog, though you might have a cat, or a hamster or other live animal. I brought a toy animal, because a real one might cause us some problems. Besides, I am going to tell you a story that starts out sad.

This is your pet. It is hit by a car. When you come home from school, your mother tells you how the car hit your dog and how she took it to the vet's office. She doesn't know if your dog is alive. Of course, you rush down to the animal doctor's office. As you go into the building you see your dog lying on a table. He isn't moving a muscle. He looks dead. You start to cry. Then you see the vet take this (the hypodermic needle) and walk over to your pet. The vet gives your dog a shot.

Then you know the dog is still alive. The doctor would not give a dead animal a shot. Your mother got the pet to the doctor in time. The shot helps save his life. You still have your pet. It's a happy story.

In that story you knew the dog was alive even though it looked dead. When the doctor gave it a shot, you knew it was alive because dead animals do not need shots.

In the Bible story for today Jesus is talking to people who did not believe that dead people are raised from their graves to live again. Some people believe that when you die your life is over. You are gone. But you didn't go anywhere.

But Jesus says that because He died for us and because He rose from the dead, we all will be raised from the dead. Jesus pointed to proof of the resurrection. He said, "And Moses clearly proves that the dead are raised to life. In the passage about the burning bush he speaks of the Lord as 'the God of Abraham, the God of Isaac, and the God of Jacob.' He is the God of the living, not the dead, for to him all are alive."

When Moses asked God who He was, God said, "I am the God of Abraham, the God of Isaac, and the God of Jacob." Those people had been buried for more than 1,000 years. From our point of view, they were dead.

But to God they were not dead. He is not the God of dead people. He is the God of living people. Abraham, Isaac, and Jacob were with God. He had given them a life that would last forever.

God also promises us that when we die, we will live again. Jesus has told us He would be with us forever. But He did not stay in the grave. He is alive. So we won't stay in the grave either. We will live with Him.

You Are Safe with Jesus

The Word

Jesus said, "Don't be afraid when you hear of wars and revolutions; such things must happen first, but they do not mean that the end is near. . . . But not a single hair from your heads will be lost. Stand firm and you will save yourselves." Luke 21:9, 18, 19 (From the Gospel for the Twenty-sixth Sunday After Pentecost)

The World

A toy snake (or picture) and an aquarium.

Jesus told His followers about a lot of scary things that would happen. He said there would be wars, revolutions, earthquakes, famines, and strange things in the sky. He said people would hate us and throw us in jail. It's scary to talk about things like that. Some of us like to see dangerous things on TV, but we wouldn't want to do those things that might hurt us. So we wonder why Jesus talked about such frightening things.

To help you understand, I'll show you this snake. Of course it is not a real snake. A real poisonous snake would be dangerous. Some snakes are not dangerous, but those who don't know which are which are scared of all snakes. If this were a live, poisonous snake we would all be afraid. But you could be this close (a foot) from a poisonous snake and not be afraid. See—(put the snake in the aquarium and cover it.) Now there is no danger. You can be close to a dangerous snake in a zoo or museum and not be afraid. As long as the glass is between you and the snake, you are not in danger.

Jesus talked about scary things so we would learn that we need protection from them. Wars, earthquakes and many other scary things are real. But Jesus says we don't have to be afraid. He says, "Not a single hair from your heads will be lost. Stand firm, and you will save yourselves."

We need to know that Jesus is with us when we are in danger. Jesus does not always take the danger away. But He does put it in a cage. He puts a limit on the ways we can be hurt. He is like the glass that protects us from the snake. He comes between us and all dangers.

As long as Jesus is with us, we are safe. He does not tell us that nothing bad will happen to us. Those who love Jesus can also be hurt in war and in accidents. We also have pain and sorrow. But Jesus wants us to know those things will not destroy us. Even if we are killed, not a hair from our head will be lost because Jesus will raise us from the dead.

We can be afraid of many things when we are afraid to die. Many people want to make us afraid by telling us we will die, or that Jesus is coming in a way that will scare us. But when Jesus comes, He will come to take us to be with Him. He will not frighten us. He will fill us with joy. And even if we die, we need not be afraid. Jesus already died to take the pain from our death. You are safe with Jesus.

What God Wants You to Do

The Word
In a story Jesus told, He said: "Before he left, he called his ten servants and gave them each a gold coin and told them, 'See what you can earn with this while I am gone.'" Luke 19:13 (From the Gospel for the Twenty-seventh Sunday After Pentecost)

The World
Three children, a scissors, crayon, roll of tape, piece of paper, and a box.

I want to put my name on this box so everyone will know it is mine. But I don't want to write on the box; so I'll put my name on a paper and tape the paper to the box. Will you help me?

(Give one child the scissors, another the crayon, and the third the tape.)

My piece of paper is too big. I need only a small piece; so I'll have to cut off a piece. Will you cut off a small piece of paper for me? (Hand the paper to the child with the crayon. Discuss why that child cannot cut the paper. But what could the child do? Help the child write your name on one end of the paper.)

Now my name is on the paper, but it's still too big. If I want the paper cut, who can help me? Of course, you can help because you have the scissors. (Let the child cut the paper.) Will you also tape it to the box? You would need help, wouldn't you? Whoever has the tape will help. (Let the third child tape the name to the box.) Now the job is done.

I gave each of you something so all of you could help me. But each had to help in a different way; because I gave you different tools to use. Remember I gave the scissors to you, and the crayon to you, and the tape to you. Each of you could tell what I wanted you to do, by seeing which tool I gave you.

God also asks us to help Him in different ways. We know what He wants us to do by the tools He has given us to use. Our Bible reading comes from a parable Jesus told. A man gave his servants money to invest. He expected them to earn money with the money. Some did use the money. Others only kept the money and returned it with no profit.

Jesus tells this story to help us understand how we can help God. We are not to say what we would do if we had gifts God has not given us. The person with the scissors could say that he could write better than the one with the crayon—because he doesn't have the crayon. We can talk about what we would do if we had lots of money, or could sing well, or draw well, or speak well—as long as we are asked to do those things.

But God does not ask you what you would do with tools that you do not have. He does ask you what you are going to do with those things He has given you. God's most important gift to you is His Son who is your Savior. What do you do with the gift of Christ? Do you believe in Him and love Him? Do you share that love and faith with others?

Think of other gifts God has given you: your smile, kind words, happiness. Whatever you have that is good is a gift from God. By looking at what God has given you, you will know what God wants you to do to help Him.

The King Who Was Here Will Come Back

The Word
Above Him [Jesus on the cross] were written these words: "This is the King of the Jews." And [one of the criminals] said to Jesus, "Remember me, Jesus, when You come as King!" Luke 23:38, 42 (From the Gospel for the Last Sunday After Pentecost)

The World:
A lunchpail or sack and a peanut butter and jelly sandwich.

If you watched your mother pack a lunch for you for school or for an all-day hike, you would know what you were going to have to eat. If she put this peanut butter and jelly sandwich in your lunchpail, you would know at lunchtime that you would eat the same sandwich she originally packed. You wouldn't worry that it would be just a piece of plain bread. You would not expect a big hamburger. A peanut butter and jelly sandwich went into the lunch pail and that is what will come out.

We can also know what kind of King will come to judge us and rule over us on the final day of the earth—because we know the kind of King who came to earth to be our Savior long ago. The same Jesus who lived on this earth over 1,900 years ago will come back again to take us to be in heaven with Him.

Our Bible reading tells us about Jesus who came long ago. It says He was nailed to a cross. Those who killed Him put a sign above His head. It said, "This is the King of the Jews." He was dying in a shameful and painful way. The people around Him hated Him. Yet He was called a King. Anyone could look like a king if he wore a fancy robe and a crown on his head. But only Jesus could be a King while He was nailed to a cross, while He was suffering and dying for the sins of the world.

One of the criminals who was dying on the cross next to

Jesus recognized Him as King. He said, "Remember me, Jesus, when you come as King." That man knew that the same King who was dying would come back.

Some people think that when Jesus comes to judge the world He will take everyone to heaven. They want to have a King come who will forget about all sin. But Jesus said that sin must be punished. He said that anyone who does not believe in Him cannot be a part of Him. Jesus says that those who deny Him will go to hell. And the same Jesus who left will be the one who will return.

Others are afraid to talk about their death, when they will be judged, or the time when Jesus will return to judge everyone. They are afraid that Jesus will punish them for all their sins. But remember—the same One who was here before will come back. Jesus who died to pay for your sins will come back to take you to be with Him forever. He will say that no one can punish you for your sins. Why not? You believe in Him, and He has already taken the punishment for you.

It is important for you to know Jesus as your King now. When you see how He loved and helped people, you will look forward to seeing Him again when He comes to be your King.